BIG LITTLE
Early Sequencing Skills
by Marilynn G. Barr

Reproduce and cut out this award for children as they master their sequencing skills.

LAB20134
BIG LITTLE
by Marilynn G. Barr

Published by: Little Acorn Books™
Originally published by: Monday Morning Books, Inc.

Entire contents copyright © 2013 Little Acorn Books™

Little Acorn Books
PO Box 8787
Greensboro, NC 27419-0787

Promoting Early Skills for a Lifetime™

Little Acorn Books™
is an imprint of Little Acorn Associates, Inc.

http://www.littleacornbooks.com

Permission is hereby granted to reproduce student materials in this book for non-commercial individual or classroom use. *School-wide or system-wide use is expressly prohibited.

ISBN 978-1-937257-23-1

Printed in the United States of America

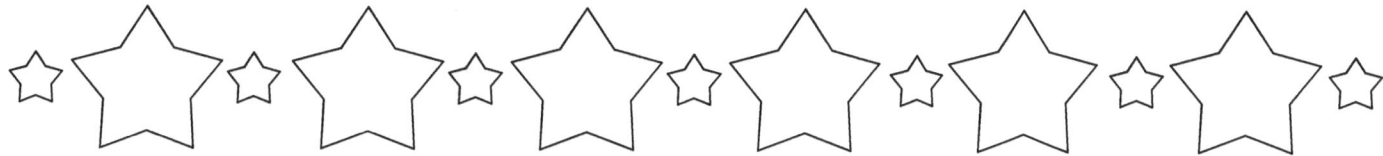

Big Little
Contents

Introduction... 4
    Big Little Activities
    Big Little Story Props
    Big Little Books
    Big Little Match Boards
    Big Little Flannel Boards
    Big Little Displays
    Big Little How Many? Chart
    Big Little Memory Card Game
    Alphabet and Number Skills Practice

Big Little Activities
    I See Small, Medium, and Large Balloons 7
    I See Kites on the Right and on the Left 9
    I See Big Stars 11
    I See Leaves on Top, Middle, and Bottom 13
    I See Small Worms 15
    I See Flowers in a Row 17
    I Know What Comes Next 19
    I Know Which Is More 23
    I Know Which Has Fewer 25
    I Know What Is Near 27
    I Know What Is Far 29
    I Can Match Baskets....................31
    I Know Big and Little 33

Big Little Activities (continued)
    I Can Stack Big and Little Hats...........35
    I Know Top, Middle, and Bottom..........37
    I Can Nest Small, Medium, and Large Stars 39
    I Can Put the Watches in Order..........41
    Up, Up and Away 49
    How Many Bunnies? 57
    What's in the Box? 58
How Many? Chart.............................59
    Chart Cards 61

Big Little Introduction

Make readiness skills practice fun with activities found in Big Little. Big Little is part of our Super School Skills series. This book deals with sequencing and concepts such as big, medium, and little. Children color, cut out, and glue objects: in a row, by pattern, and in order. Activities also feature color, shape, and size recognition. Matching, sorting, sequencing, and counting practice are also addressed. Telling time and alphabetical order are also included. Each activity is designed to help children develop fine motor skills through coloring, cutting, and pasting. For opposites and spatial skills practice try our resource Up Down. Scribble Scribble features early writing and Snip Snip focuses on early cutting skills practice.

Assembly, materials, and alternate use options are listed at the bottom of each activity page. Children can glue on pom poms, sequins, beans, rice, and cereal Os. Glitter pens can also be used to transform pages into works of art, book pages, displays, or props.

I See... activities provide color recognition, cutting exercises, and matching practice. Directions prompt children to color, cut out, choose, then glue objects on illustrated match boards. I Know... activities reinforce sequencing, counting, coloring, cutting, and following directions.

Introduce children to counting, charting, and tallying information. Display an enlarged How Many? Chart and cards (pp. 59-64) for a whole class activity. The charts and cards can also be reproduced for children to make take-home folders.

Big Little Activities

Provide children with crayons, scissors, and glue to complete the activities. Two-page activities include patterns to cut out and glue on match boards. When children complete activities, invite each child to tell what is in his or her picture. Encourage children to refer to the color and spatial relationships between objects. For example: There is a green star in front of the moon.

Options at the bottom of each activity page list alternate materials and uses. Provide children with additional materials to create textured displays and more.

Big Little Story Props

Provide each child with a construction paper square and large craft stick. When activities are completed, have each child cut out and glue his or her finished activity to a construction paper square. Then glue or staple a large craft stick to the back to form a prop.

Big Little Books

Provide children with construction paper squares, crayons, markers, scissors, and glue. Have children cut out and glue finished activities to construction paper squares to form book pages. Have children decorate construction paper covers for their books. Punch two holes along the left margin of each child's cover and book pages. Cut, lace, and tie a length of yarn or ribbon through the holes to form a book.

Big Little Match Boards

Enlarge, reproduce, color, and cut out each set of I See... cutouts and match boards. Tape or glue an envelope to the back of each match board for cutouts storage. Place the match boards in a center for individual or buddy skills practice.

Big Little Flannel Boards

Reproduce and color cutouts. Glue felt to the back of each cutout. Trim away excess felt. Measure, cut, and glue felt to a large sheet of corrugated board to make a flannel board. Cut out and glue a simple tree, house, bush, lake, and clouds on the flannel board. Store the cutouts in a basket. Place the board and basket of cutouts in a skills practice center. Children can practice matching, sequencing, and attaching cutouts to the left, right, above, below, next to, near, and far on the flannel board.

Big Little Displays

Provide optional materials listed at the bottom of activity pages. Have children decorate, then cut out and glue the pages on colored construction paper squares to make decorative displays. Hang the displays in the classroom.

Big Little How Many? Chart

Enlarge, reproduce, color, and cut out chart patterns and cards (pp. 59-64). Glue the chart to a sheet of poster board. Attach a Velcro square or magnet to each block on the chart and to the back of each object card. Choose an object for the children to help you chart and tally. Write the name of the object in the space provided on the chart. Tape or staple an envelope to the bottom of the chart to store object cards. Mount the chart to a display board. Invite children, in turn, to attach object cards to the chart. When the chart is complete, help children count and tally the results of how many sweaters, hats, gloves, or lunch boxes, are in the room.

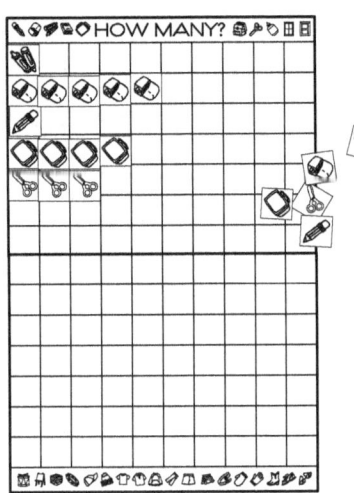

Big Little Memory Card Game

Reproduce, color, laminate, and cut apart two sets of chart cards (pp. 61-64). Store the cards in a decorated box or resealable storage bag. To play: One of two to four players shuffles, then places all the cards, face down, on a table. In turn, each child turns over two cards. If there is a match, the child takes the cards. If there is no match, the cards are turned face down and remain in the same locations. Play continues until all the cards are taken.

Alphabet and Number Skills Practice

Reproduce and program the backs of cutouts found throughout this book with letters, numbers, number words, or number sets for children to practice letter and number skills.

I See Small, Medium, and Large Balloons

Trace the dotted lines with your finger.
Trace the dotted lines with a crayon.
Color the small balloon red. Color the medium balloon blue.
Color the large balloon purple. Cut out the balloons.

Option: Paint each balloon.

I See Small, Medium, and Large Balloons

Glue the small balloon under the table.
Glue the large balloon next to the table.
Glue the medium balloon over the table.
Color the rest of the picture.

I See Small, Medium, and Large Balloons

I see a large balloon next to the table.
I see a small balloon under the table.
I see a medium balloon over the table.

Option: Trace the balloon outlines with a glitter pen. Color the balloons. Cut out the page along the dotted lines. Glue the page on a sheet of construction paper.

I See Kites on the Right and on the Left

Trace the dotted lines with your finger.
Trace the dotted lines with a crayon.
Color one kite red, one blue, one yellow, and one purple.
Cut out the kites.

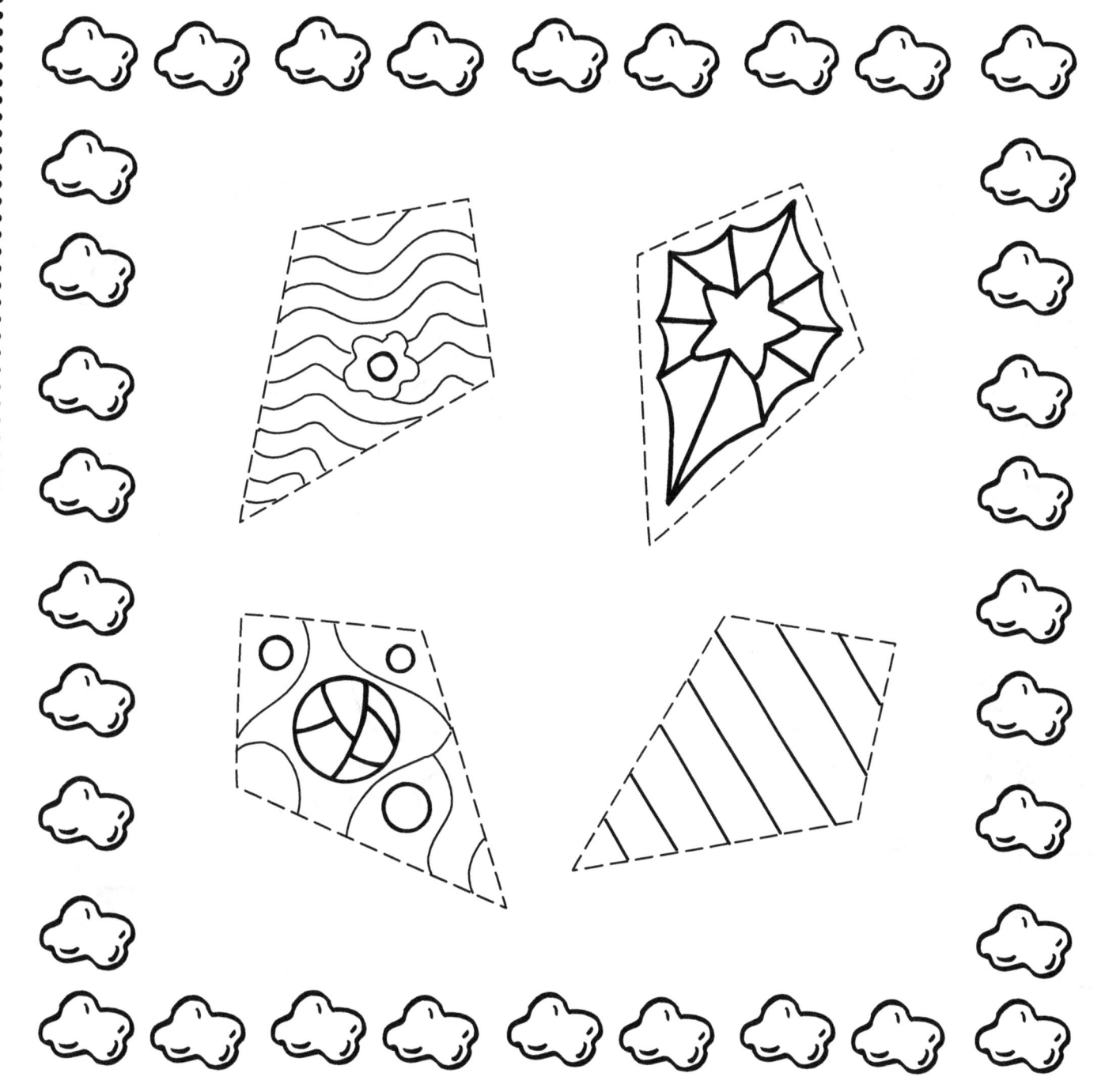

Option: Color the kites, then glue buttons on the kite cutouts.

I See Kites on the Right and on the Left

Glue the red kite on the right side of the cloud.
Glue the blue kite next to the red kite.
Glue the yellow kite on the left side the cloud.
Glue the purple kite next to the yellow kite.

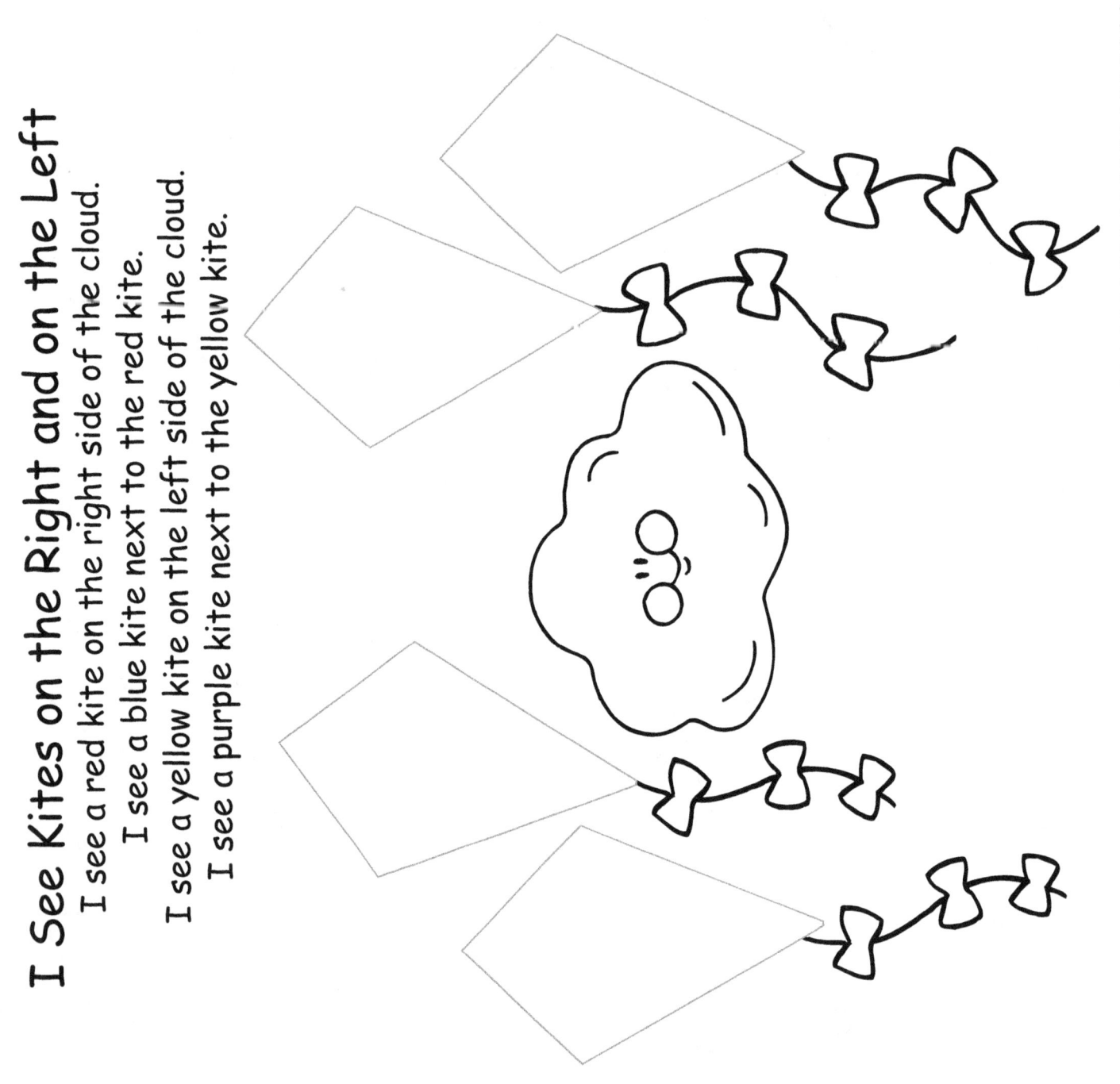

Option: Trace the kite outlines with a glitter pen. Color the kites. Cut out the page along the dotted lines. Glue the page on a sheet of construction paper.

I See Big Stars

Trace the dotted lines with your finger.
Trace the dotted lines with a crayon.
Color the biggest star yellow. Color the next biggest star orange.
Color the last star purple. Cut out the stars.

Option: Color the page, then glue sequins on the star cutouts.

I See Big Stars

Glue the biggest star on first.
Glue the next biggest star on second.
Glue the third biggest star on last.
Color the rest of the picture.

I See Big Stars

I see a big purple star.
I see a bigger orange star.
I see the biggest yellow star.

Option: Trace the star outlines with a glitter pen. Color the stars. Cut out the page along the dotted lines. Glue the page on a sheet of construction paper.

I See Leaves on Top, Middle, and Bottom

Trace the dotted lines with your finger.
Trace the dotted lines with a crayon.
Color one leaf green. Color one leaf purple. Color two leaves orange.
Cut out the leaves.

Option: Color the page, then glue dry beans on the leaf cutouts.

I See Leaves on Top, Middle, and Bottom

Glue the purple leaf at the bottom of the basket.
Glue the green leaf in the middle of the basket.
Glue the orange leaves on top of the basket.
Color the rest of the picture.

I See Leaves on Top, Middle, and Bottom

I see a purple leaf at the bottom of the basket.
I see a green leaf in the middle of the basket.
I see orange leaves at the top of the basket.

Option: Trace the leaf outlines with a glitter pen. Color the leaves. Cut out the page along the dotted lines. Glue the page on a sheet of construction paper.

I See Small Worms

Trace the dotted lines with your finger.
Trace the dotted lines with a crayon.
Color the smallest worm purple. Color the next smallest worm yellow.
Color the the last worm red. Cut out the worms.

Option: Color the page, then glue yarn or pom poms on the worms.

I See Small Worms

Glue the purple worm on the right side of the apple.
Glue the yellow worm on the left side of the apple.
Glue the red worm on the front of the apple.
Color the rest of the picture.

I See Small Worms

I see a worm in the apple.
I see a smaller worm on the left side of the apple.
I see the smallest worm on the right side of the apple.

Option: Trace the worm outlines with a glitter pen. Color the bugs. Cut out the page along the dotted lines. Glue the page on a sheet of construction paper.

I See Flowers in a Row

Trace the dotted lines with your finger.
Trace the dotted lines with a crayon.
Color one flower blue, one flower purple, and one flower orange.
Cut out the flowers.

Option: Cut and glue green yarn stems and leaves under each flower.

I See Flowers in a Row

Glue the blue flower on first.
Glue the purple flower next to the blue flower.
Glue the orange flower next to the purple flower.
Color the rest of the picture.

I See Flowers in a Row

I see blue, purple, and orange flowers.
The blue flower is first.
The purple flower is next.
The orange flower is last.

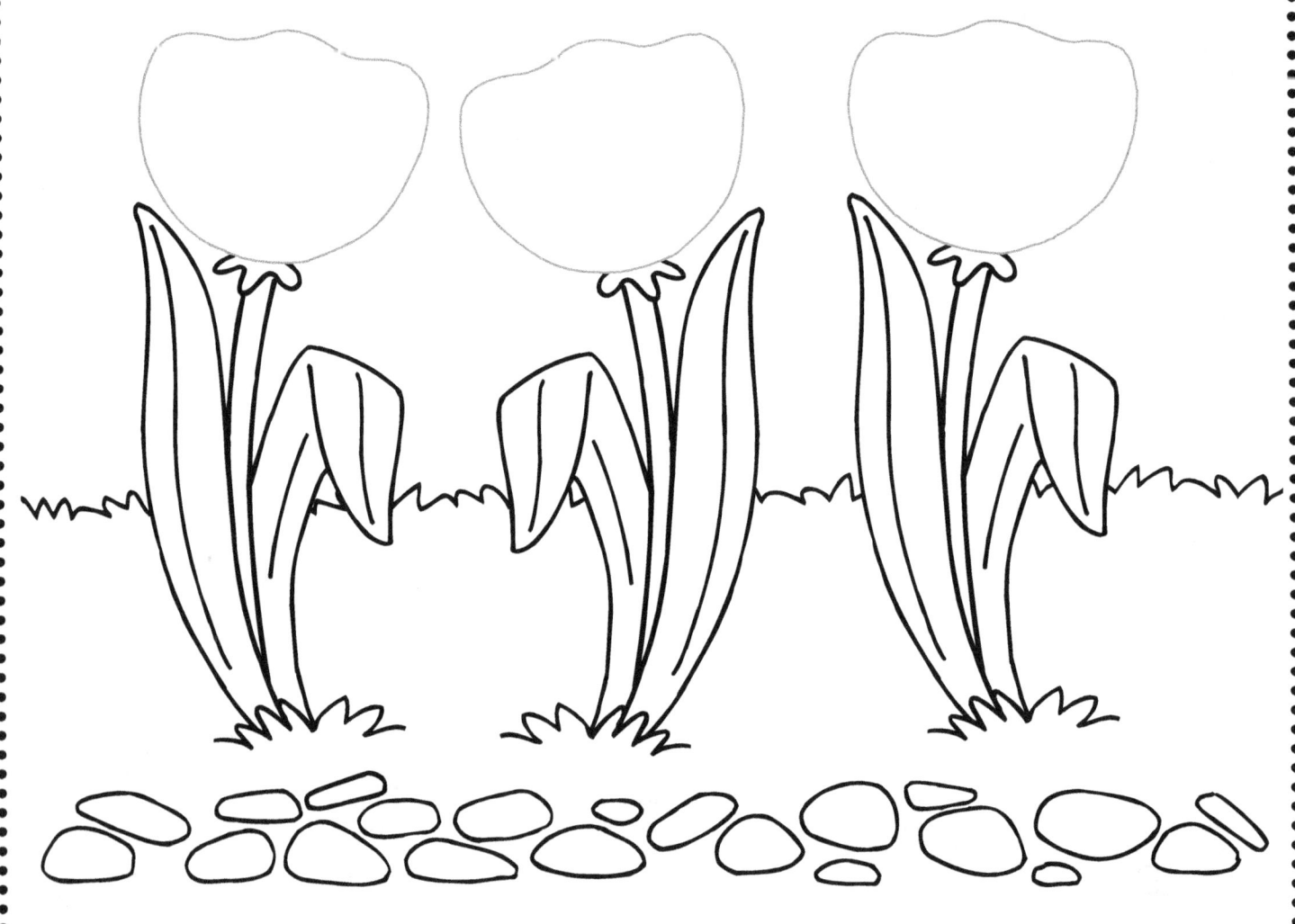

Option: Trace, cut out, and glue cloth flowers on the outlines. Cut out the page along the dotted lines. Glue the page on a sheet of construction paper.

I Know What Comes Next

Look at the beads on each necklace.
What is the pattern?
Draw the shape that comes next on the last bead.
Color the beads.

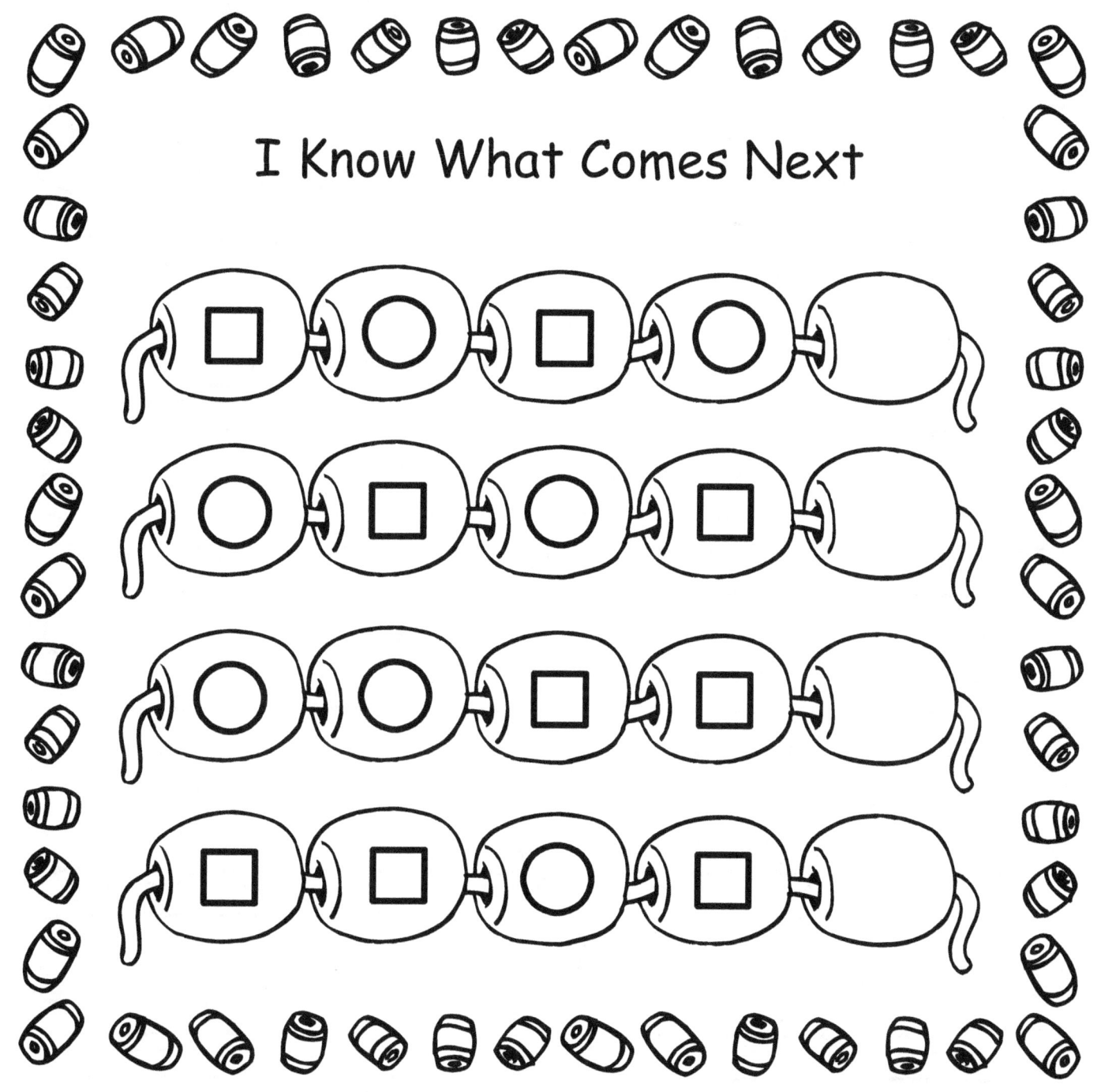

Option: Glue buttons on the circles and star stickers on the squares.

I Know What Comes Next

Look at the cups in each stack.
What is the pattern?
Draw the shape that comes next on the empty cup at the bottom.
Color the cups.

I Know What Comes Next

Option: Reproduce, color, and cut apart the cups and saucers in each stack to use as counters..

I Know What Comes Next

Look at the fish in each row.
What is the pattern?
Draw the shape that comes next on the last fish.
Color the fish.

Option: Color the fish and glue them to a sheet of construction paper. Then lightly paint green and blue waves over and around the fish.

I Know What Comes Next

Look at the turtles in each row.
What is the pattern?
Color the turtle that comes next purple.
Color the rest of the turtles.

Option: Glue one blue pom pom on each polka dot turtle. Glue one green pom pom on each checkerboard turtle.

I Know Which Is More

Look at the baskets.
Count the eggs in each basket.
Color each basket with more eggs yellow.
Color the rest of the picture.

Option: Glue different colored beans on the eggs in each basket.

I Know Which Is More

Look at the mugs.
Count the marshmallows in each mug.
Color each mug with more marshmallows blue.
Color the rest of the picture.

Option: Glue a tiny white pom pom on each marshmallow.

I Know Which Has Fewer

Look at the leaves.
Count the ladybugs on each leaf.
Color each leaf with fewer ladybugs green.
Color the rest of the picture.

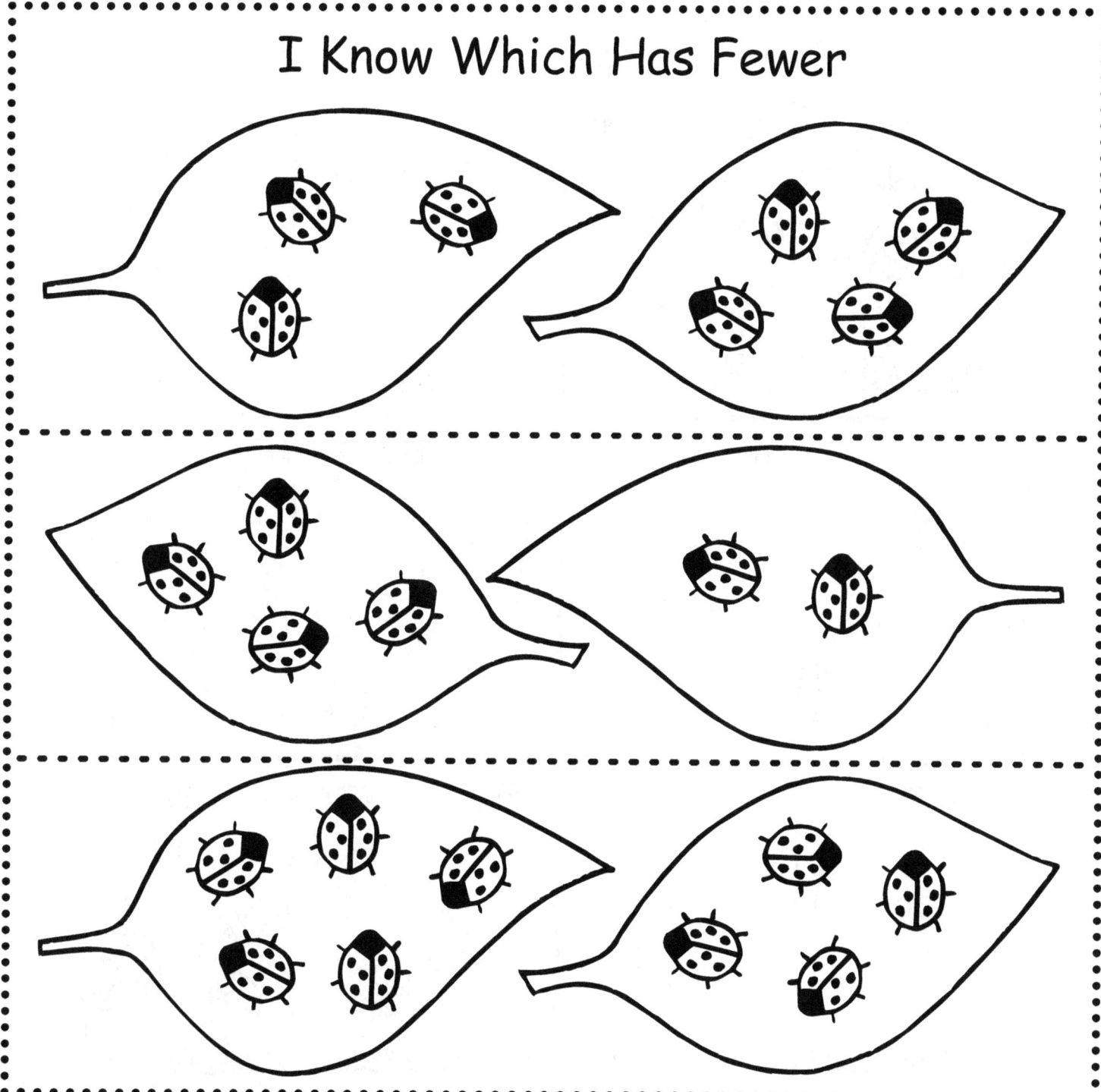

Option: Glue green yarn along the outline of each leaf.

I Know Which Has Fewer

Look at each bag.
Count the pretzels in each bag.
Color the bag with fewer pretzels brown.
Color the rest of the picture.

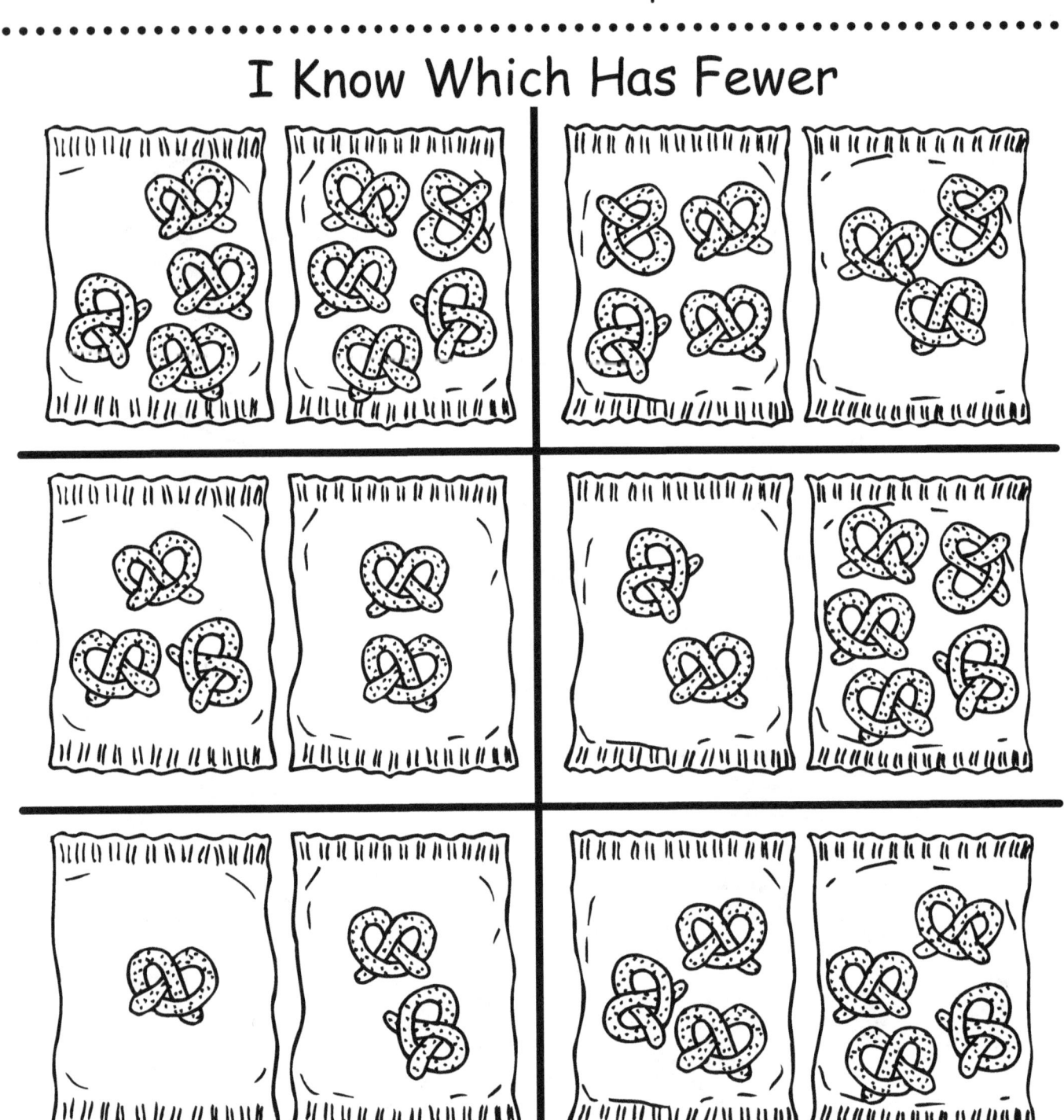

Option: Apply glue then sprinkle sand on each pretzel.

I Know What Is Near

Look at the picture.
One bird is near and one bird is far.
Color the bird that is near blue.
Color the rest of the picture.

Option: Glue beads on the berries.

I Know What Is Near

Look at the picture.
One bear is near and one bear is far.
Color the bear that is near pink.
Color the rest of the picture.

Option: Draw flowers on the hill. Draw a sun in the sky.

I Know What Is Far

Look at the picture.
One car is near. One car is far. One car is in between.
Color the car that is far red.
Color the rest of the picture.

Option: Decorate the cars with glue and glitter.

I Know What Is Far

Look at the picture.
One bunny is near and one bunny is far.
Color the bunny that is far pink.
Color the rest of the picture.

I Know What Is Far

Option: Color the little carrots orange. Color the big carrot yellow.

I Can Match Baskets

Color the baskets with triangles orange.
Color the baskets with stars purple.
Color the baskets with circles pink.
Color the baskets with squares blue.
Cut out the baskets.

Option: Cut out and glue baskets in a row to make a spring picture.

I Can Match Baskets

Glue the triangle baskets in the upper left corner.
Glue the square baskets in the lower left corner.
Glue the star baskets in the upper right corner.
Glue the circle baskets in the lower right corner.

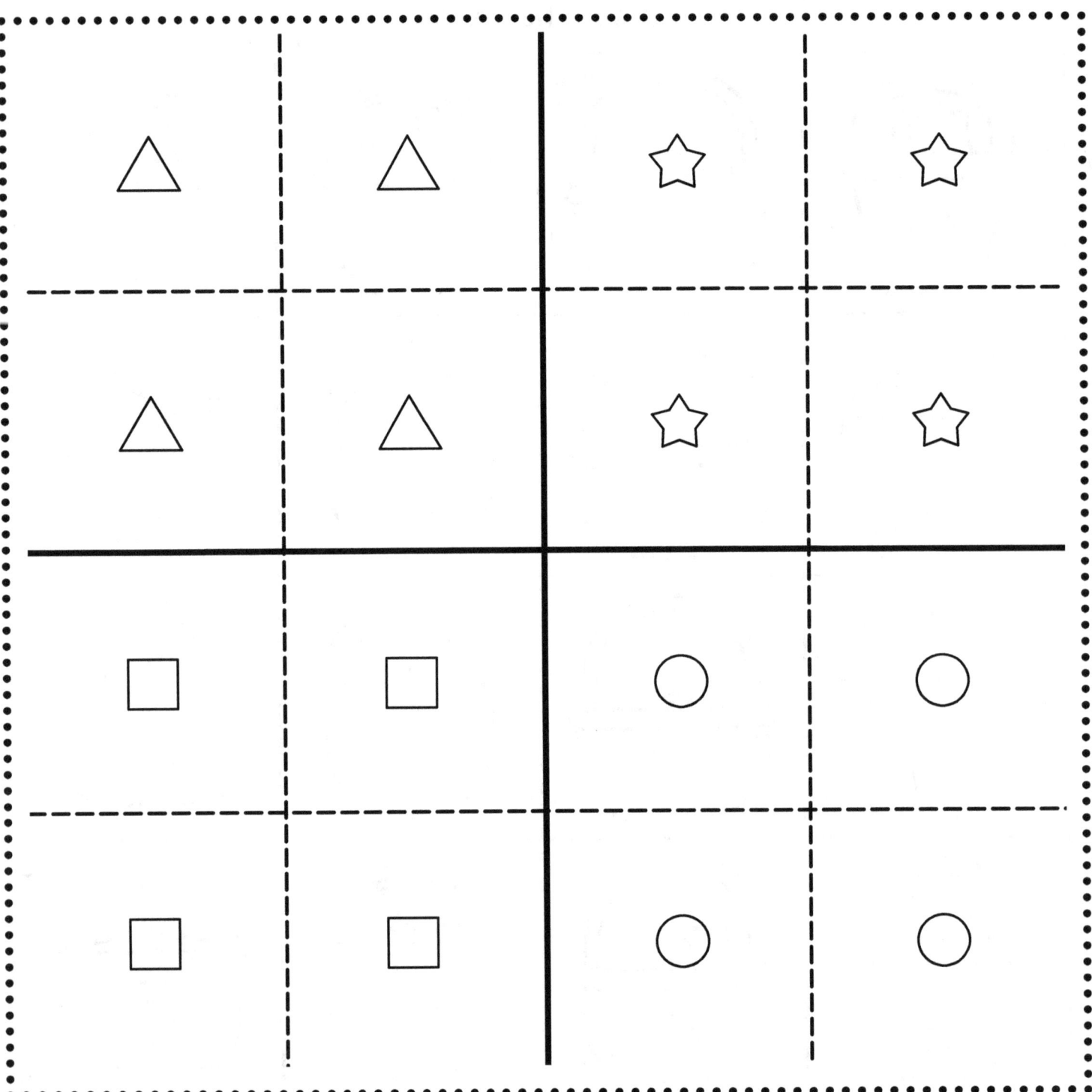

Option: Sort baskets by style.

I Know Big and Little

Color the little mittens orange.
Color the big mittens purple.
Cut out the mittens.

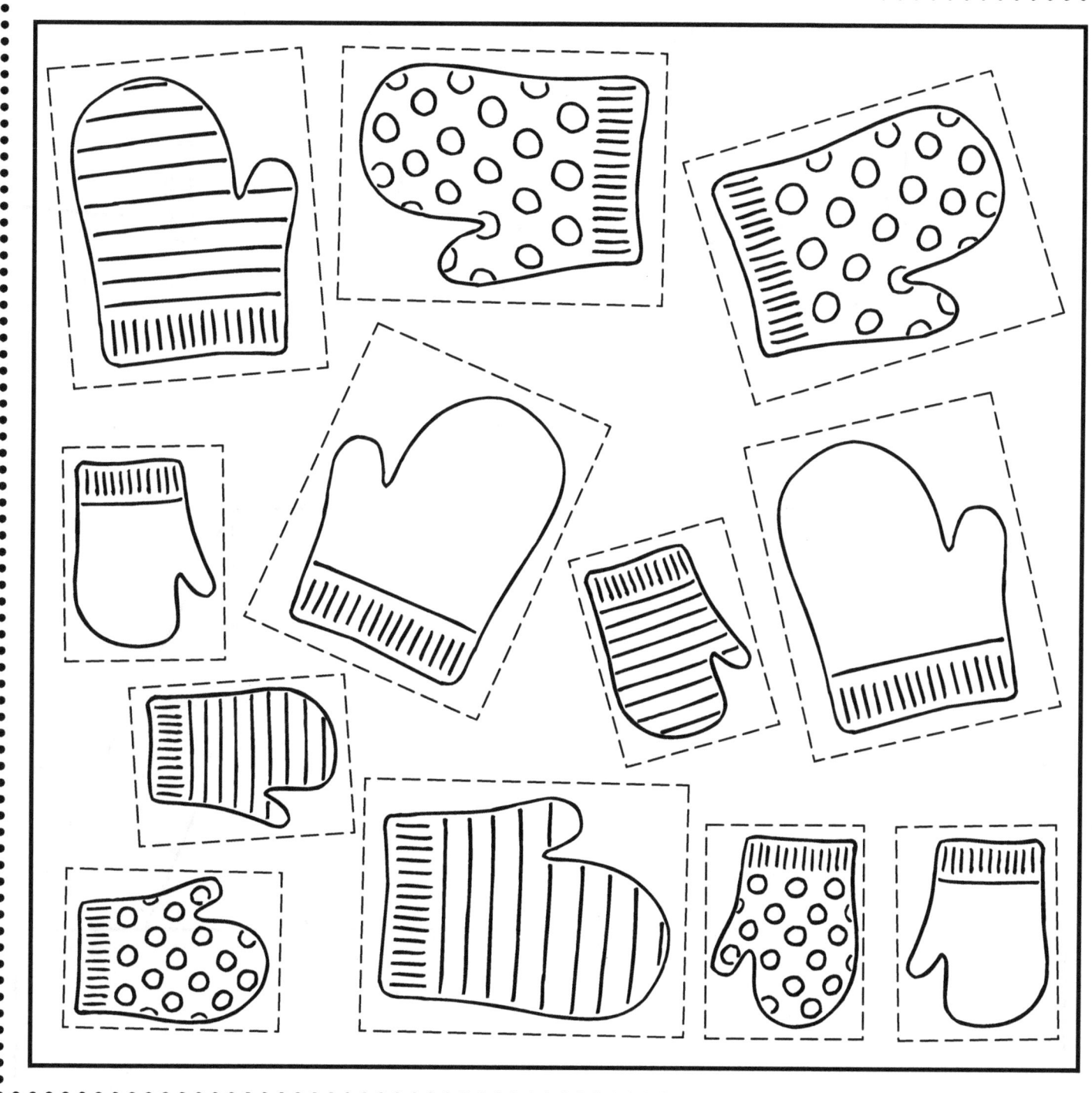

Option: Cut and glue yarn on each mitten.

I Know Big and Little

Glue four little mittens on the clothesline.
Glue two big mittens in the box.

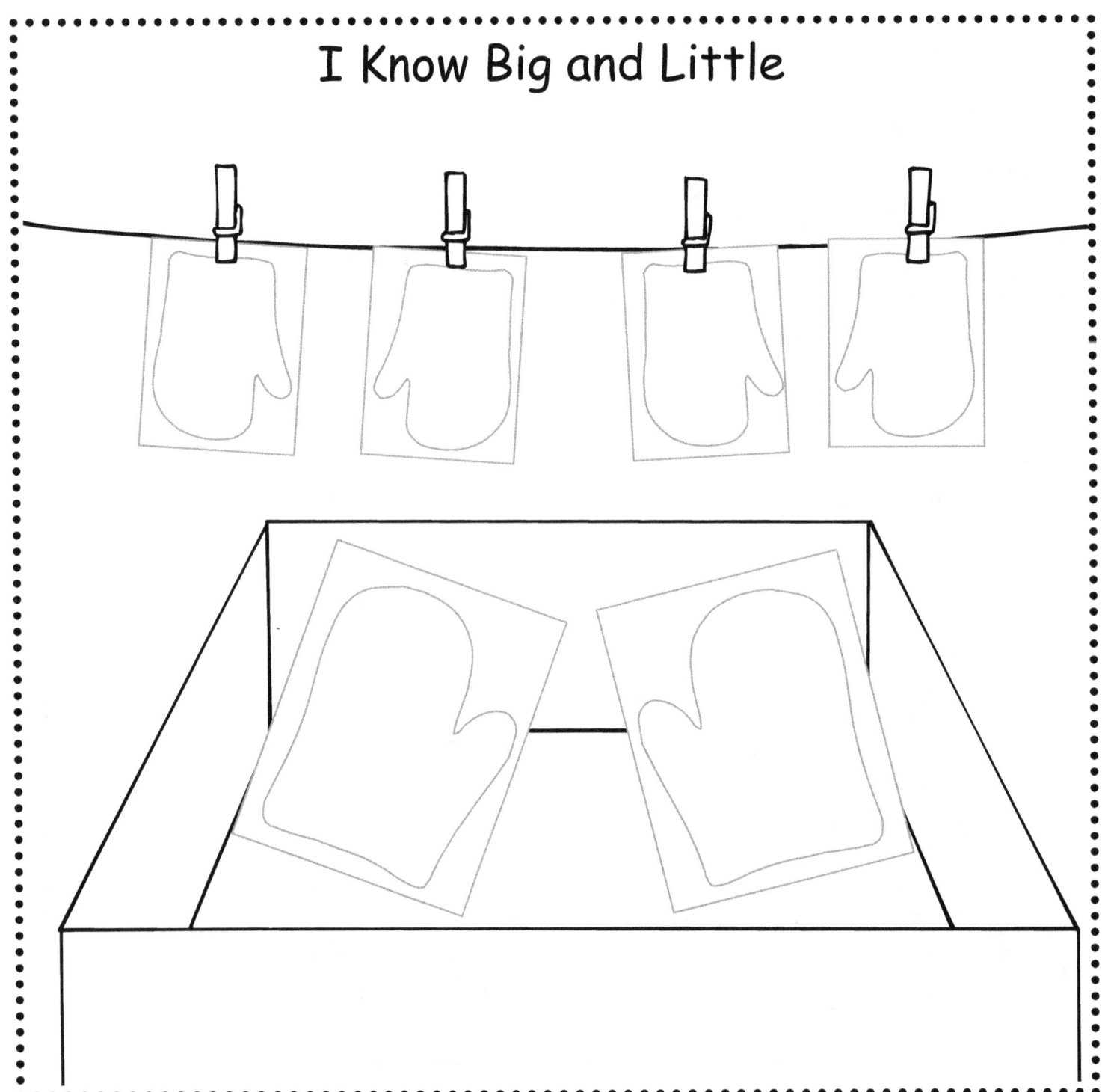

Option: Color the mitten outlines. Then glue a button on each mitten.

I Can Stack Big and Little Hats

Color the little hats red and blue.
Color the big hats yellow and green.
Cut out the hats.

Option: Decorate the hats with glue and glitter. Glue craft feathers on the hats.

I Can Stack Big and Little Hats

Stack and glue the big hats on the left.
Stack and glue the little hats on the right.

Option: Cut out and glue gift wrap to each hat box.

I Know Top, Middle, and Bottom

Trace the shapes.
Color the shapes.
Cut out the shapes.

Option: Trace and cut out the shapes from felt or cloth scraps.

I Know Top, Middle, and Bottom

Glue the small shapes at the top.
Glue the large shapes at the bottom.
Glue the medium shapes in the middle.

I Know Top, Middle, and Bottom

top

middle

bottom

Option: Draw circles at the top. Draw squares in the middle. Draw triangles at the bottom..

I Can Nest Small, Medium, and Large Stars

Trace the stars.
Color the stars.
Cut out the stars.

Option: Trace the stars with glitter pens. Glue a button in the center of each star.

I Can Nest Small, Medium, and Large Stars

First, glue on the large stars.
Then glue the medium stars on top of the large stars.
Next, glue the small stars on top of the medium stars.
Color the rest of the picture.

Option: Glue yellow yarn around each set of nested stars.

I Can Nest Small, Medium, and Large Stars

Trace the watches.
Color the watches.
Cut out the watches.

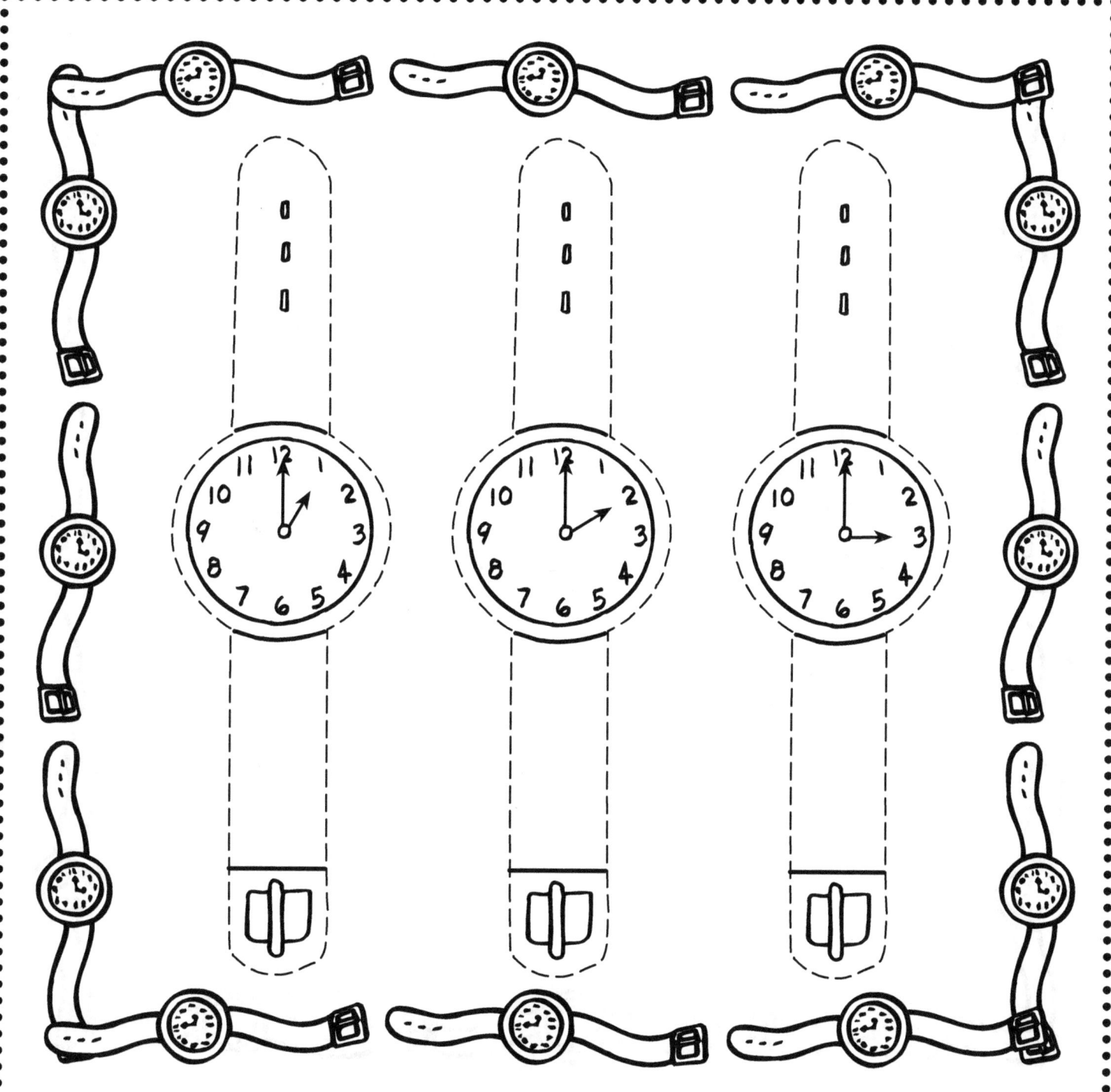

Option: Trace, cut out, and glue gift wrap bands on each watch.

I Can Put the Watches in Order

Look at the number on each watch outline.
Glue the watch with the matching time on each outline.
Color the picture.

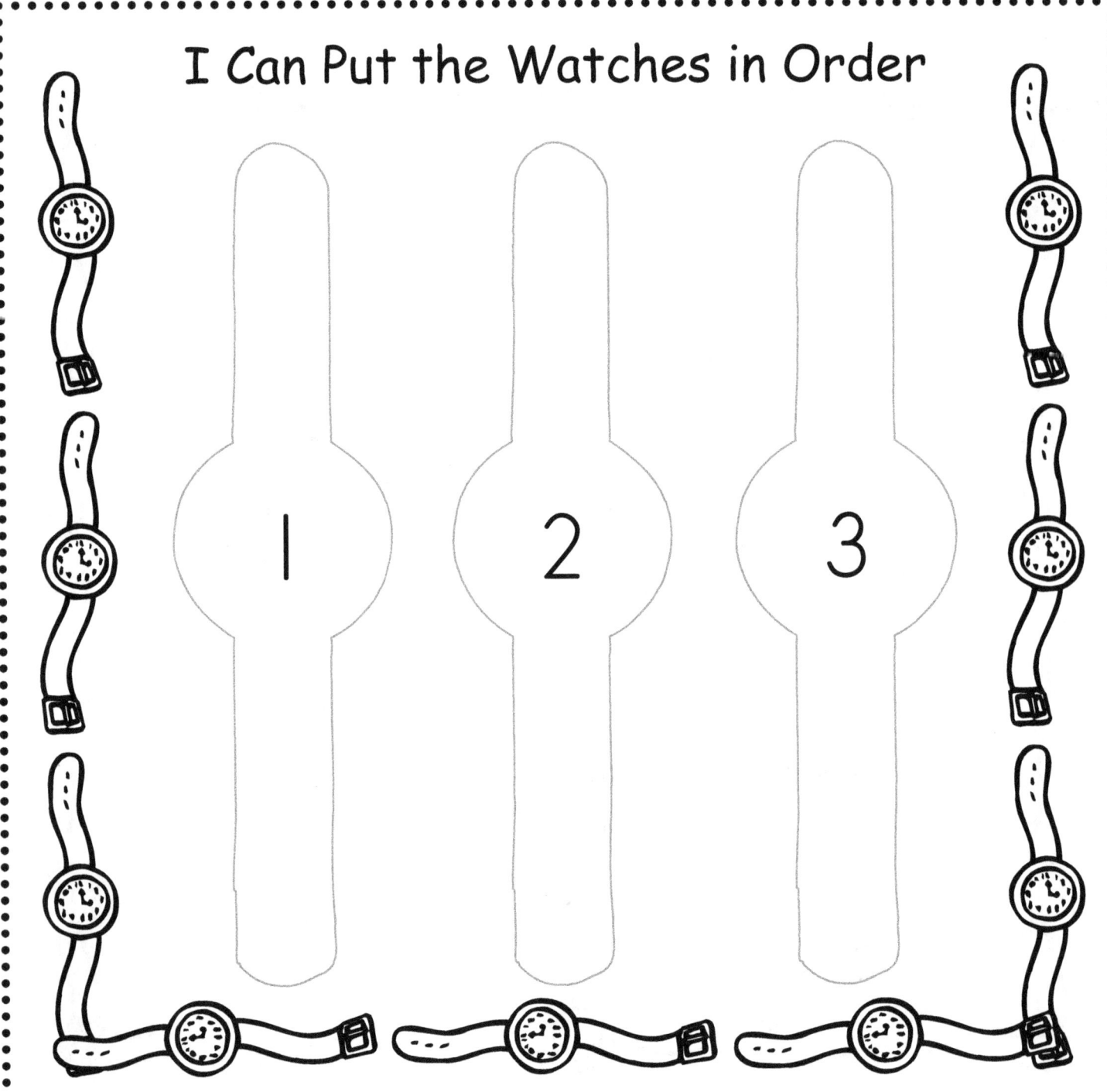

Option: Trace, cut out, and decorate the watch outlines to make bracelets. Secure bracelets with tape.

I Can Put the Watches in Order

Trace the watches.
Color the watches.
Cut out the watches.

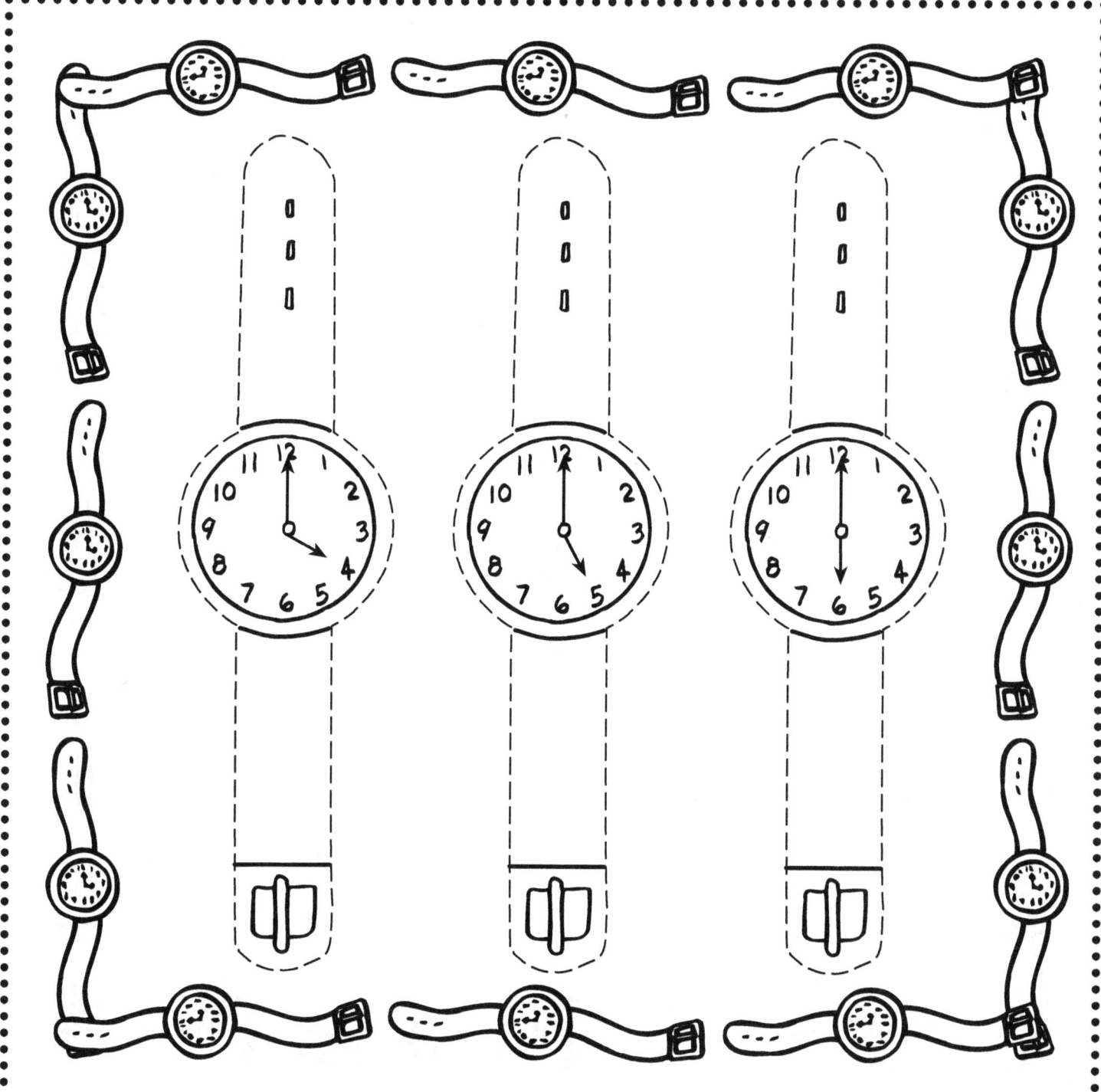

Option: Trace, cut out, and glue fabric bands on each watch.

I Can Put the Watches in Order

Look at the number on each watch outline.
Glue the watch with the matching time on each outline.
Color the picture.

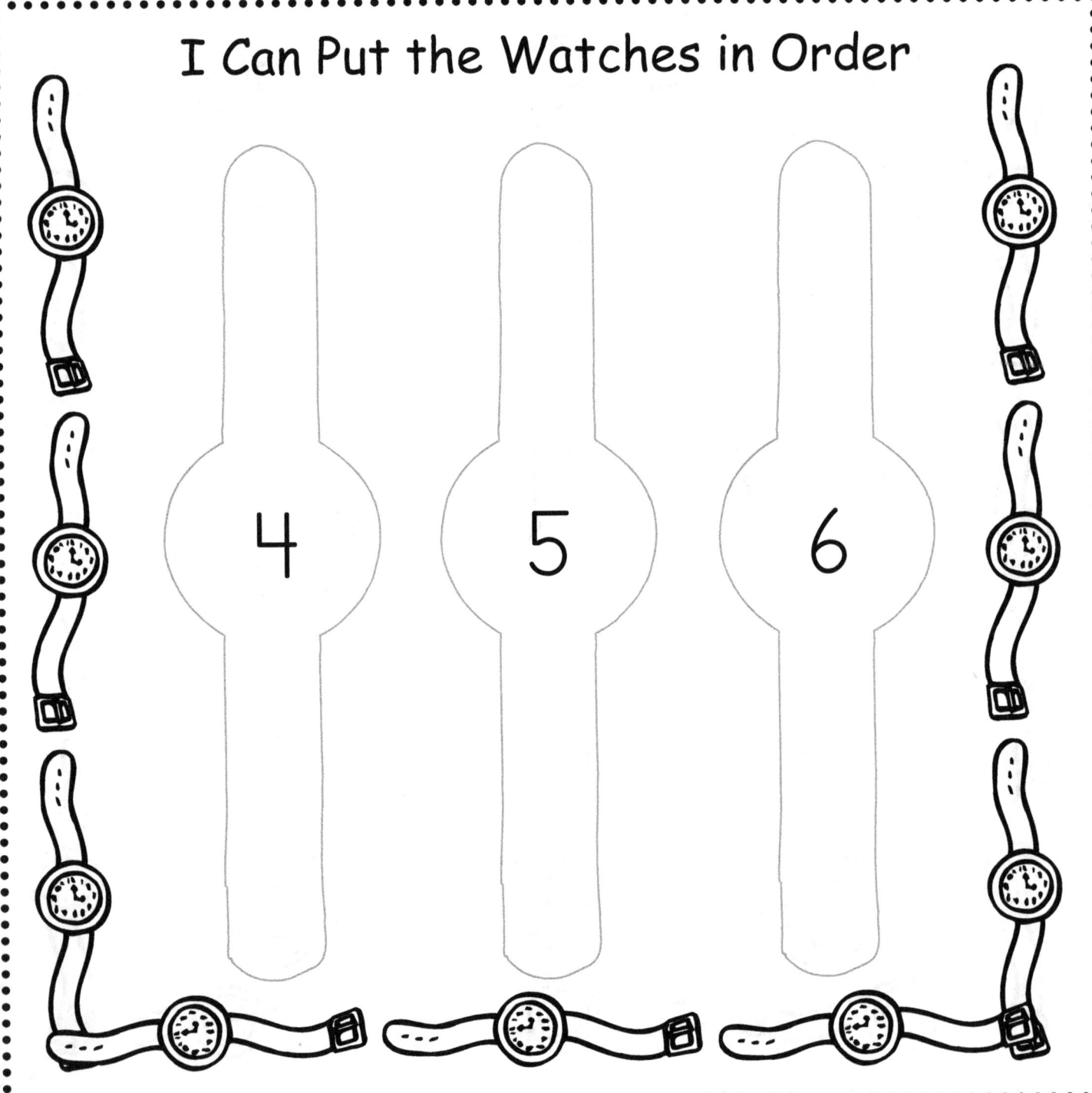

Option: Trace, cut out, and decorate the watch outlines with glitter and glue.

I Can Put the Watches in Order

Trace the watches.
Color the watches.
Cut out the watches.

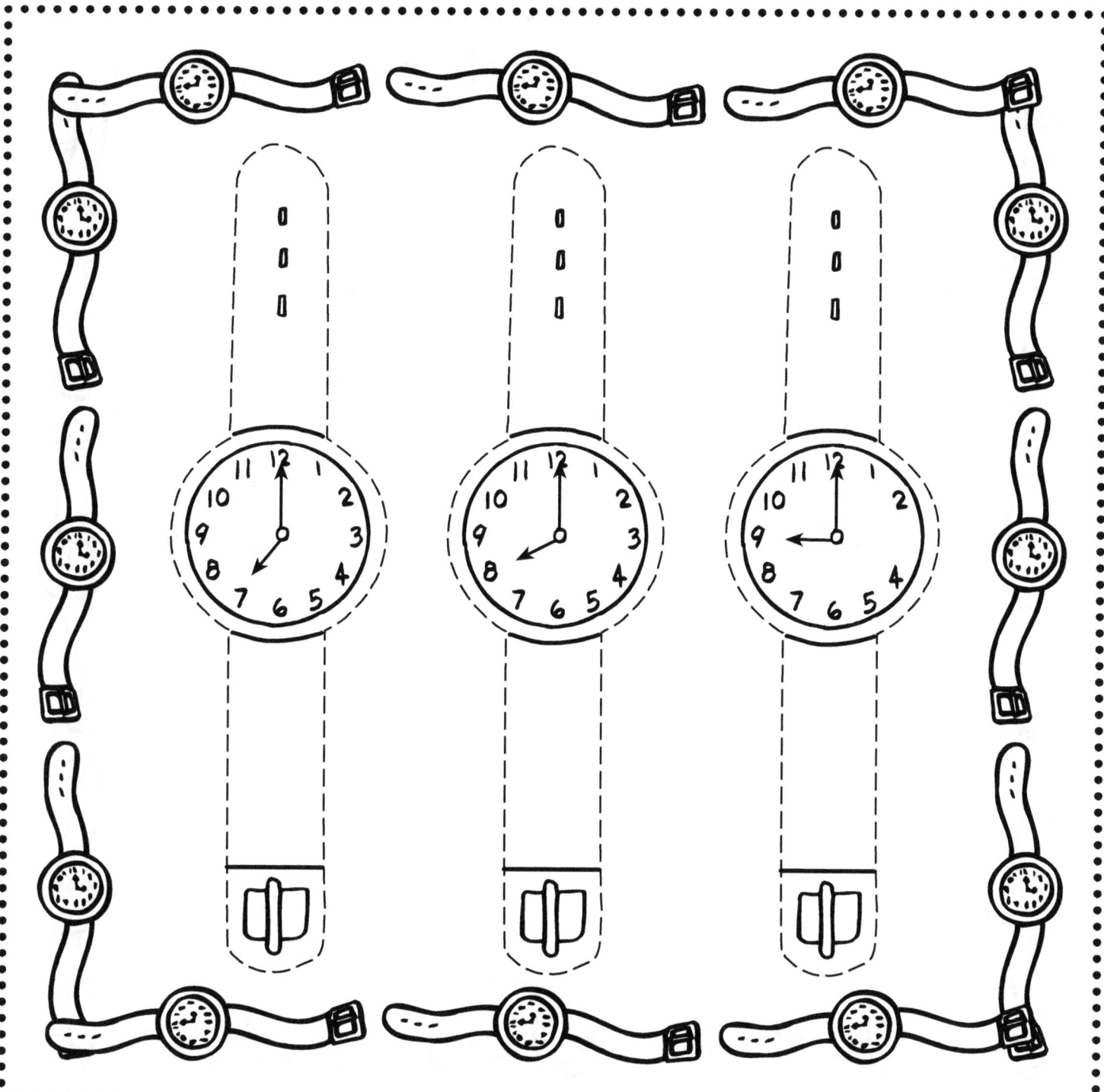

Option: Trace, cut out, and glue aluminum foil bands on each watch.

I Can Put the Watches in Order

Look at the number on each watch outline.
Glue the watch with the matching time on each outline.
Color the picture.

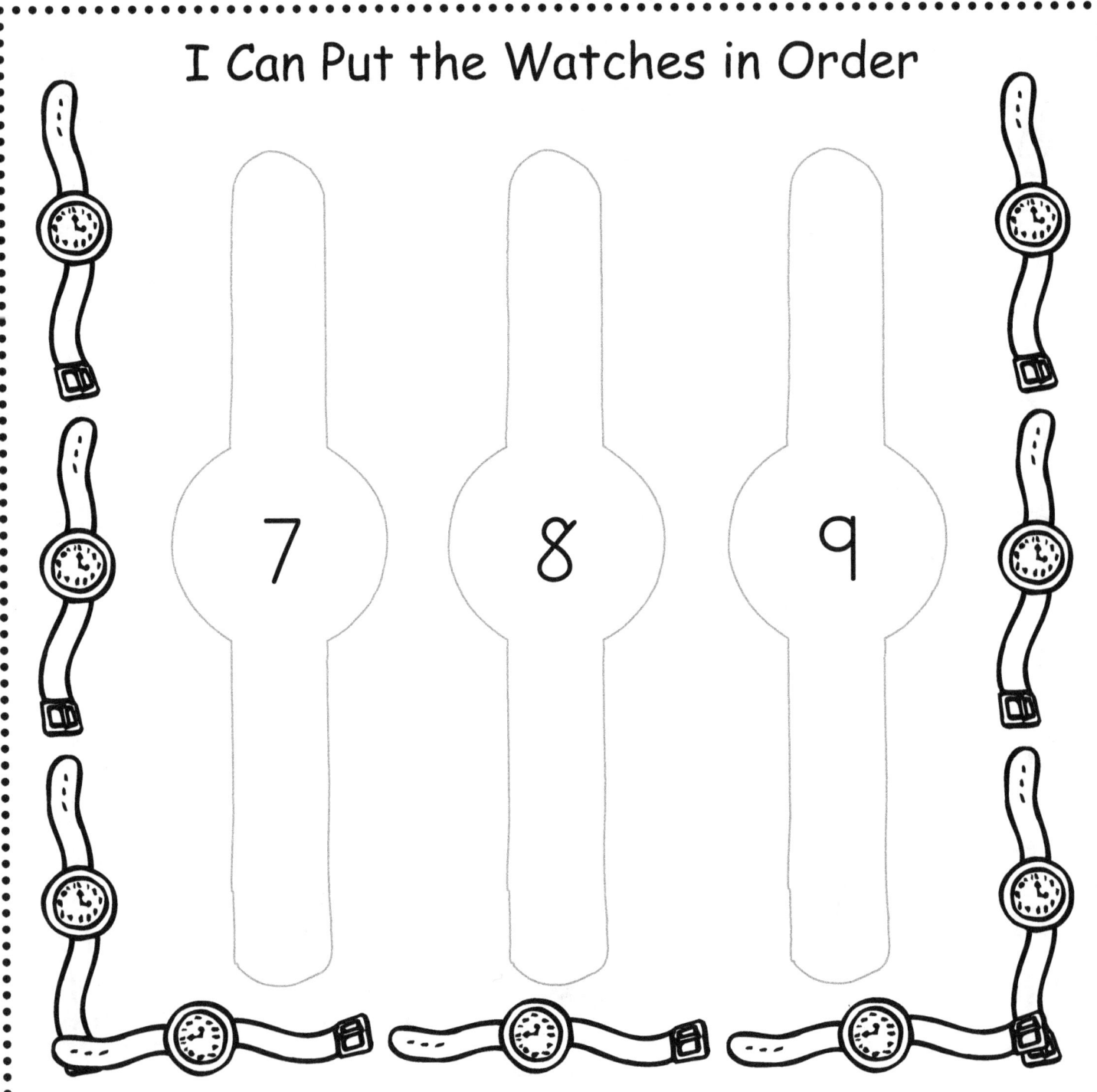

Option: Glue the matching number of pom poms on each outline.

I Can Put the Watches in Order

Trace the watches.
Color the watches.
Cut out the watches.

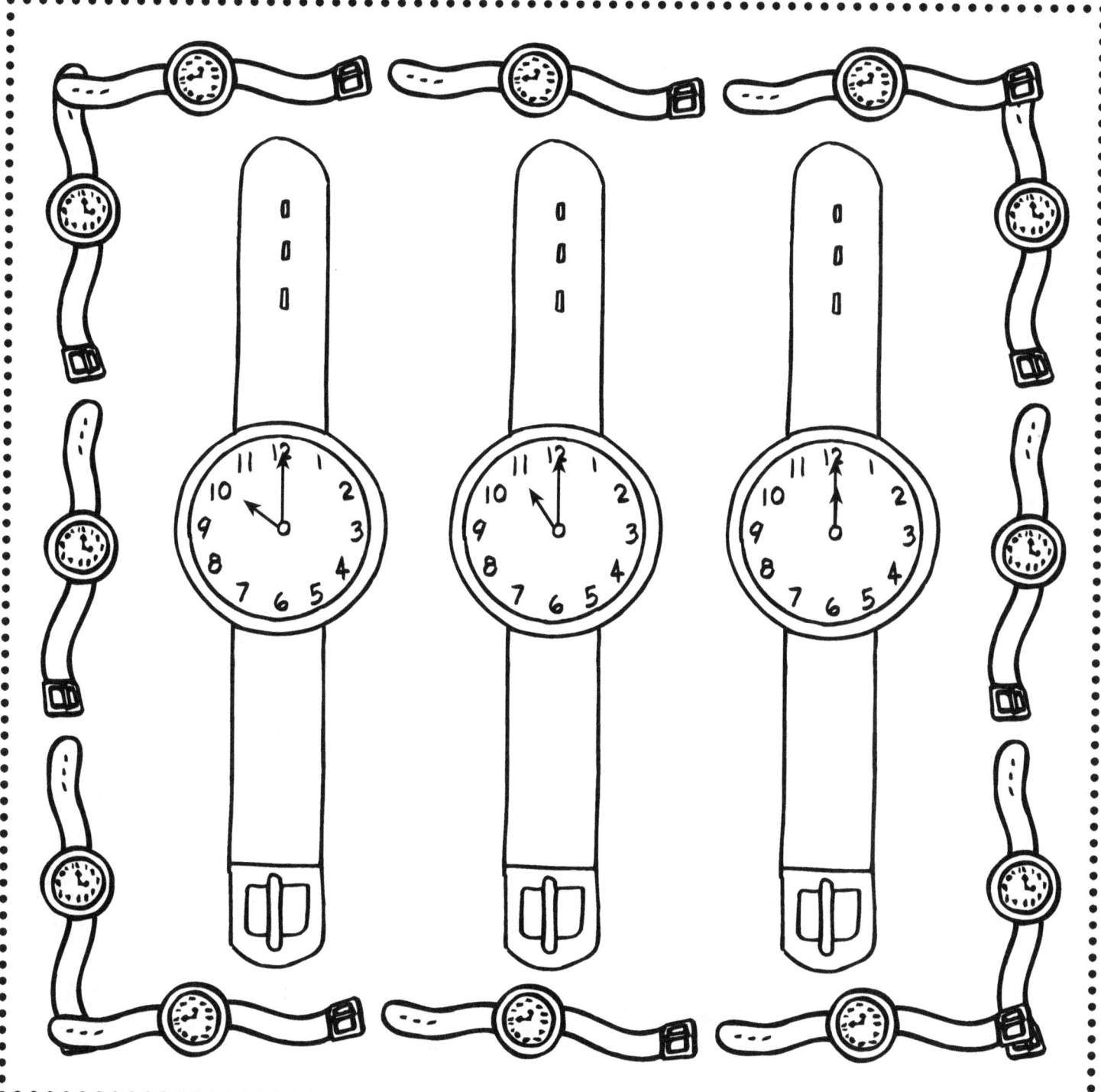

Option: Trace, cut out, and glue newspaper comics bands on each watch.

I Can Put the Watches in Order

Look at the number on each watch outline.
Glue the watch with the matching time on each outline.
Color the picture.

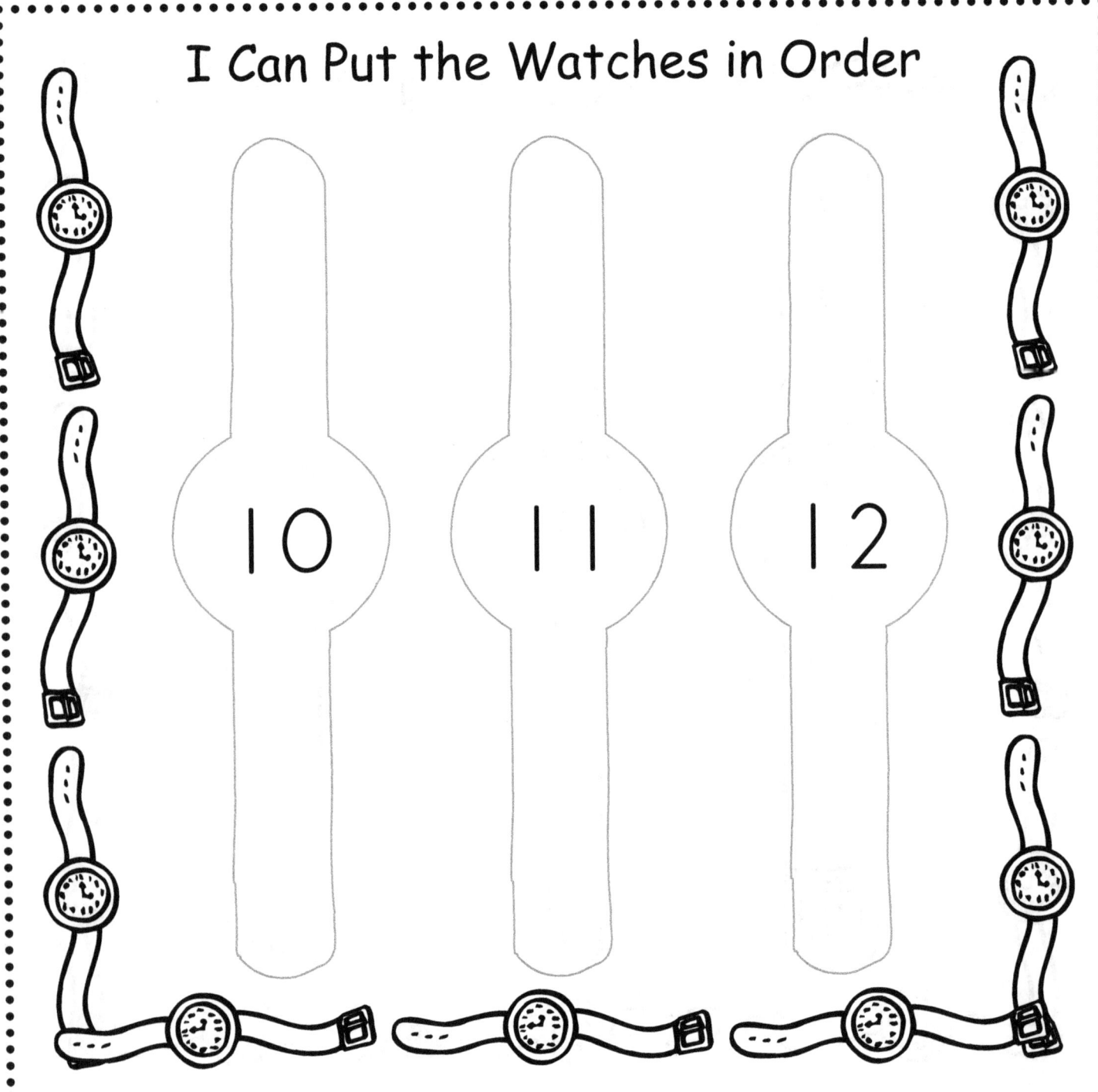

Option: Trace, cut out, and decorate the watch outlines to make bracelets. Glue a photograph in the center of each bracelet. Secure bracelets with tape.

I Can Put the Watches in Order

Trace the letters.
Color the hot air balloons.
Cut out the hot air balloons.

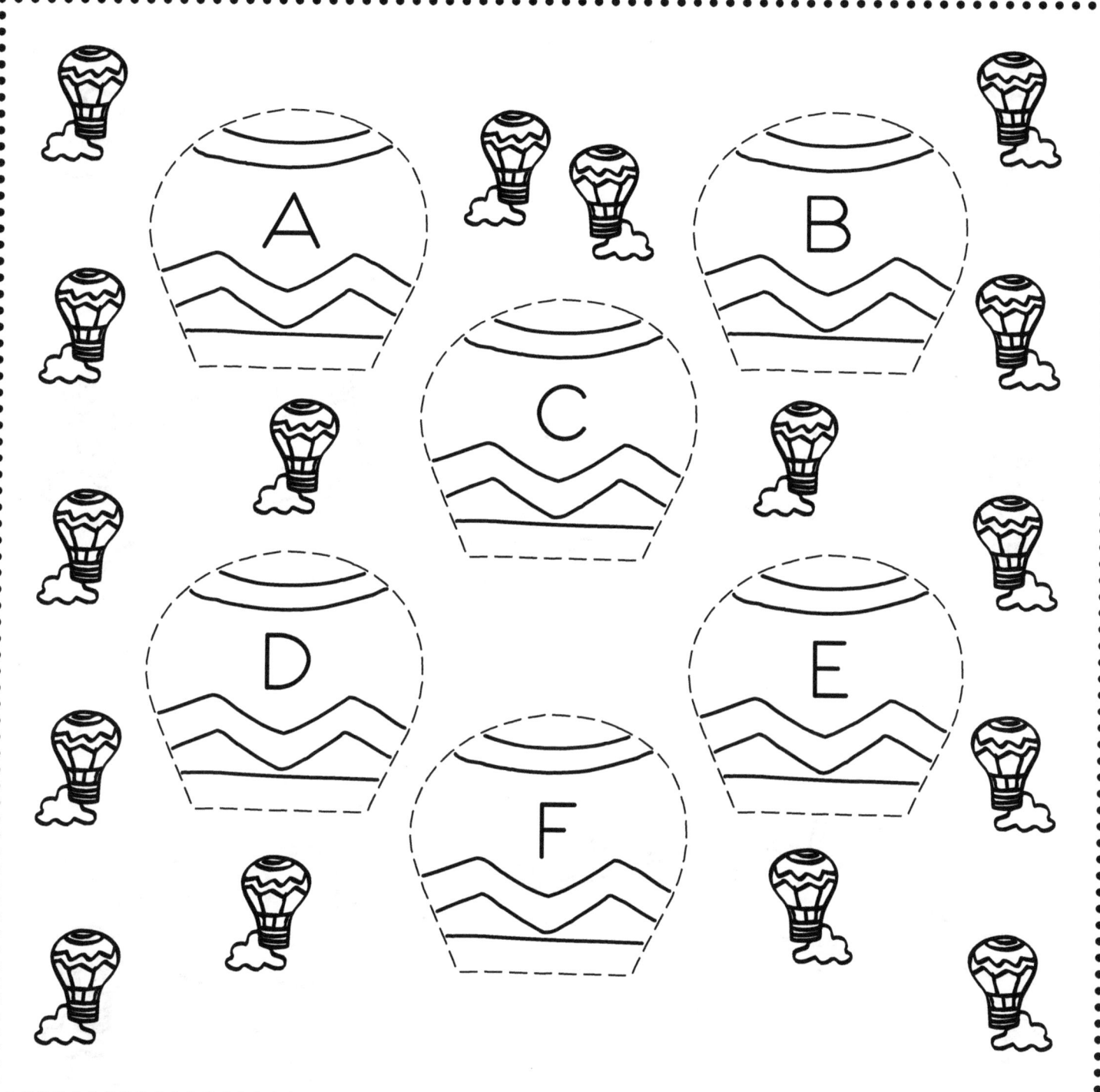

Option: Reproduce construction paper hot air balloons. Use crayons to color the balloons.

Up, Up and Away

Glue the matching hot air balloon over each basket.
Color the picture.

Option: Write the matching uppercase letter, then decorate each balloon outline.

Up, Up and Away

Trace the letters.
Color the hot air balloons.
Cut out the hot air balloons.

Option: Reproduce a construction paper sheet of hot air balloons. Use glitter pens to color the balloons.

Up, Up and Away

Glue the matching hot air balloon over each basket.
Color the picture.

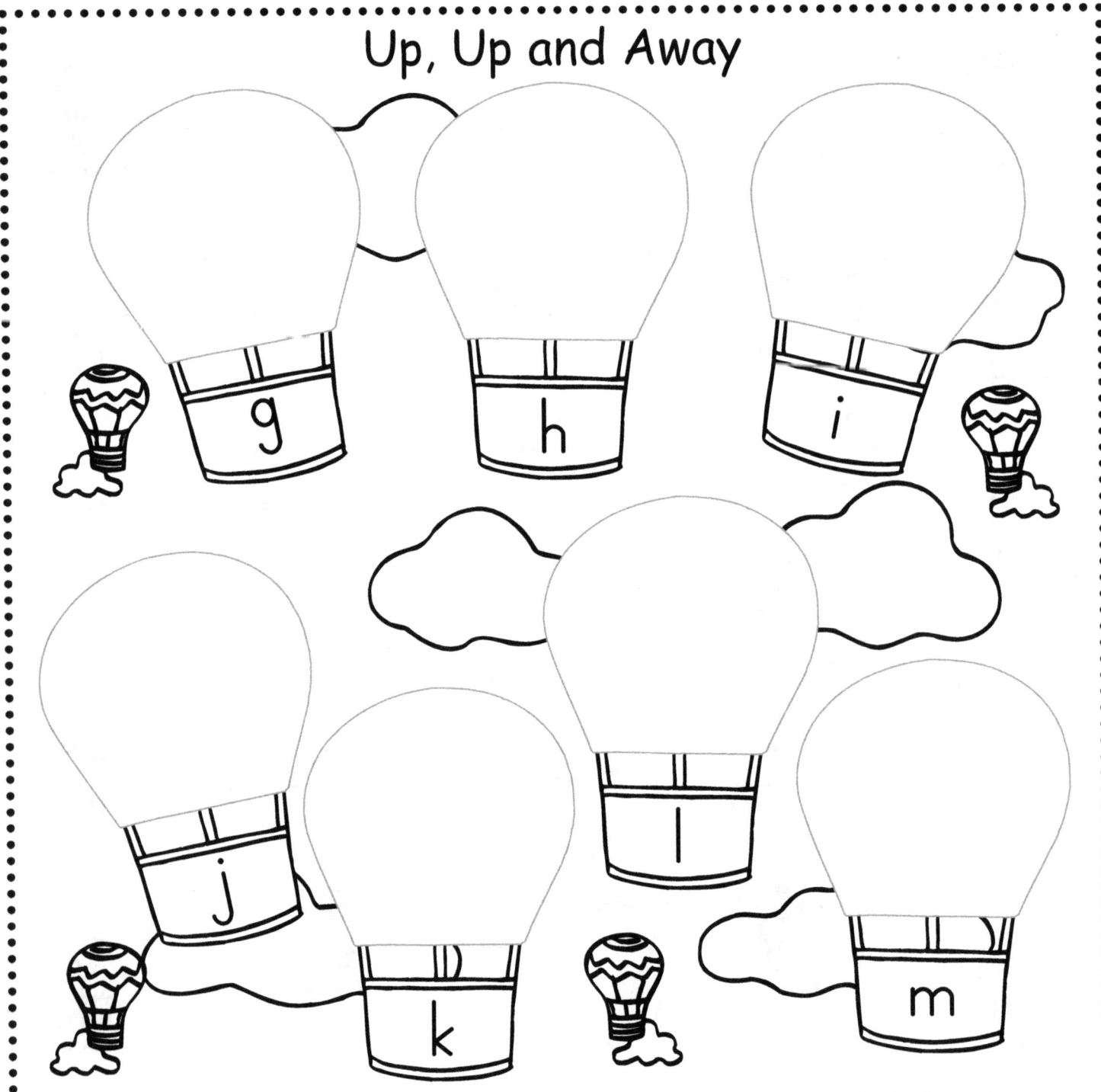

Option: Write the matching uppercase letter on each balloon outline.

Up, Up and Away

Trace the letters.
Color the hot air balloons.
Cut out the hot air balloons.

Option: Reproduce a construction paper sheet of hot air balloons. Use markers to color the balloons.

Up, Up and Away

Glue the matching hot air balloon over each basket.
Color the picture.

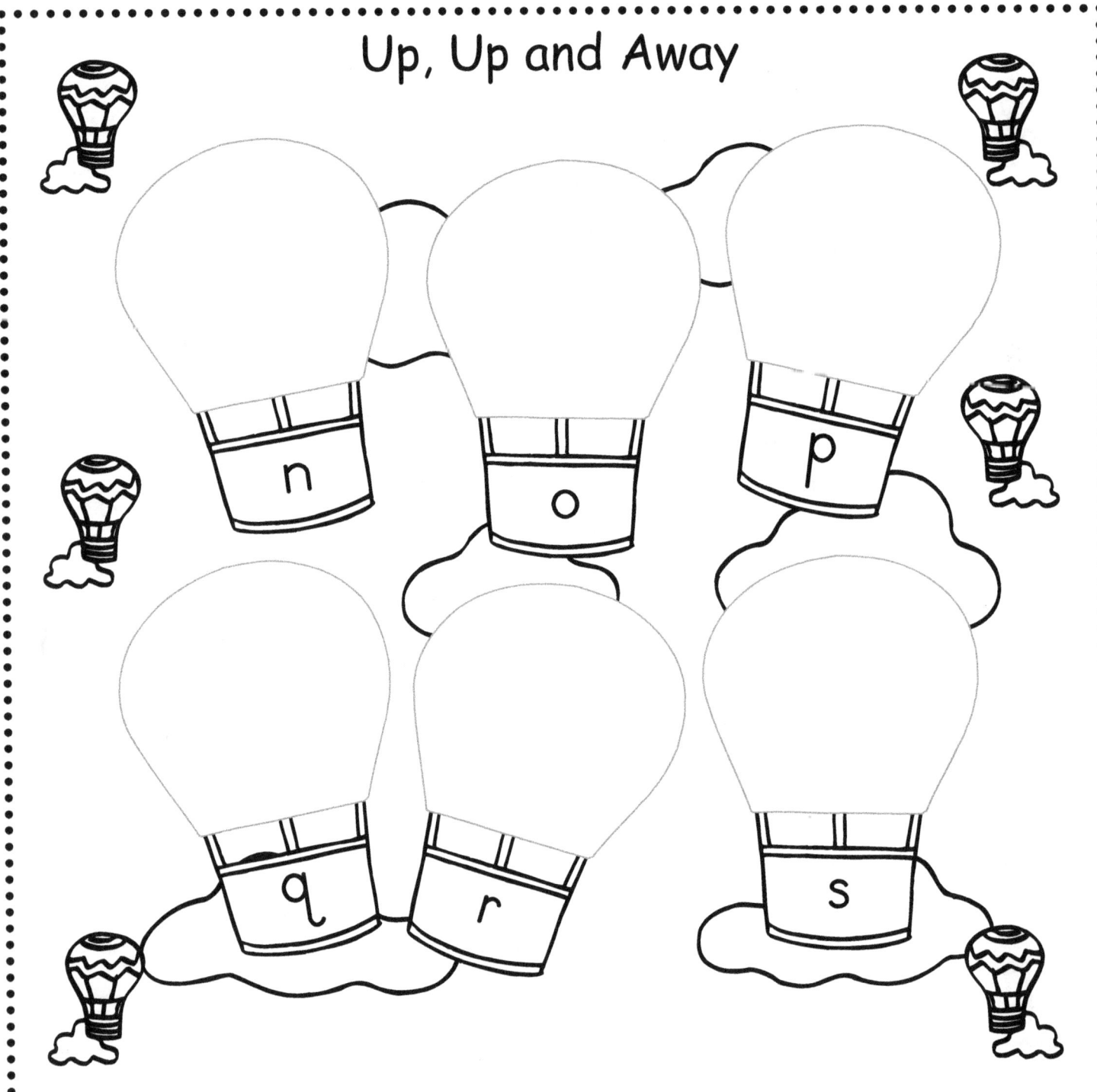

Option: Write the matching uppercase letter on each balloon outline.

Up, Up and Away

Trace the letters.
Color the hot air balloons.
Cut out the hot air balloons.

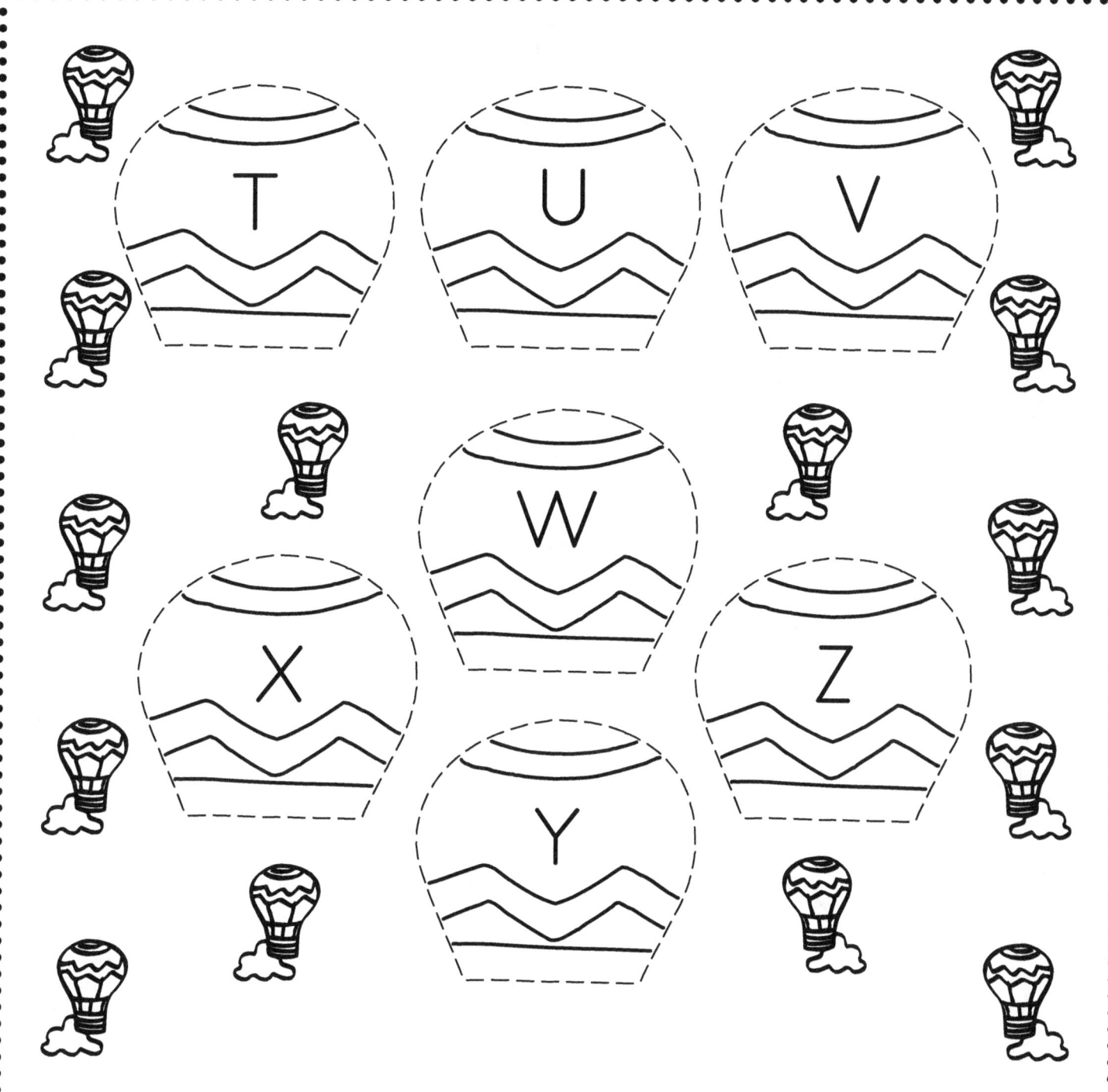

Option: Reproduce a construction paper sheet of hot air balloons. Use glitter pens to color the balloons.

Up, Up and Away

Glue the matching hot air balloon over each basket.
Color the picture.

Option: Write the matching uppercase letter on each balloon outline.

How Many Bunnies?

Look at the bunnies.
Color the large bunnies blue.
Color the small bunnies pink.
Color the medium bunnies orange.

Option: Glue a cotton ball or a tuft of cotton on each rabbit.

What's in the Box?

Look at the objects in the box.
Color the large objects orange.
Color the small objects purple.
Color the medium objects green.

Option: Color, cut out, and glue the box on a construction paper square.

Up, Up and Away

HOW MANY?

Chart

Chart

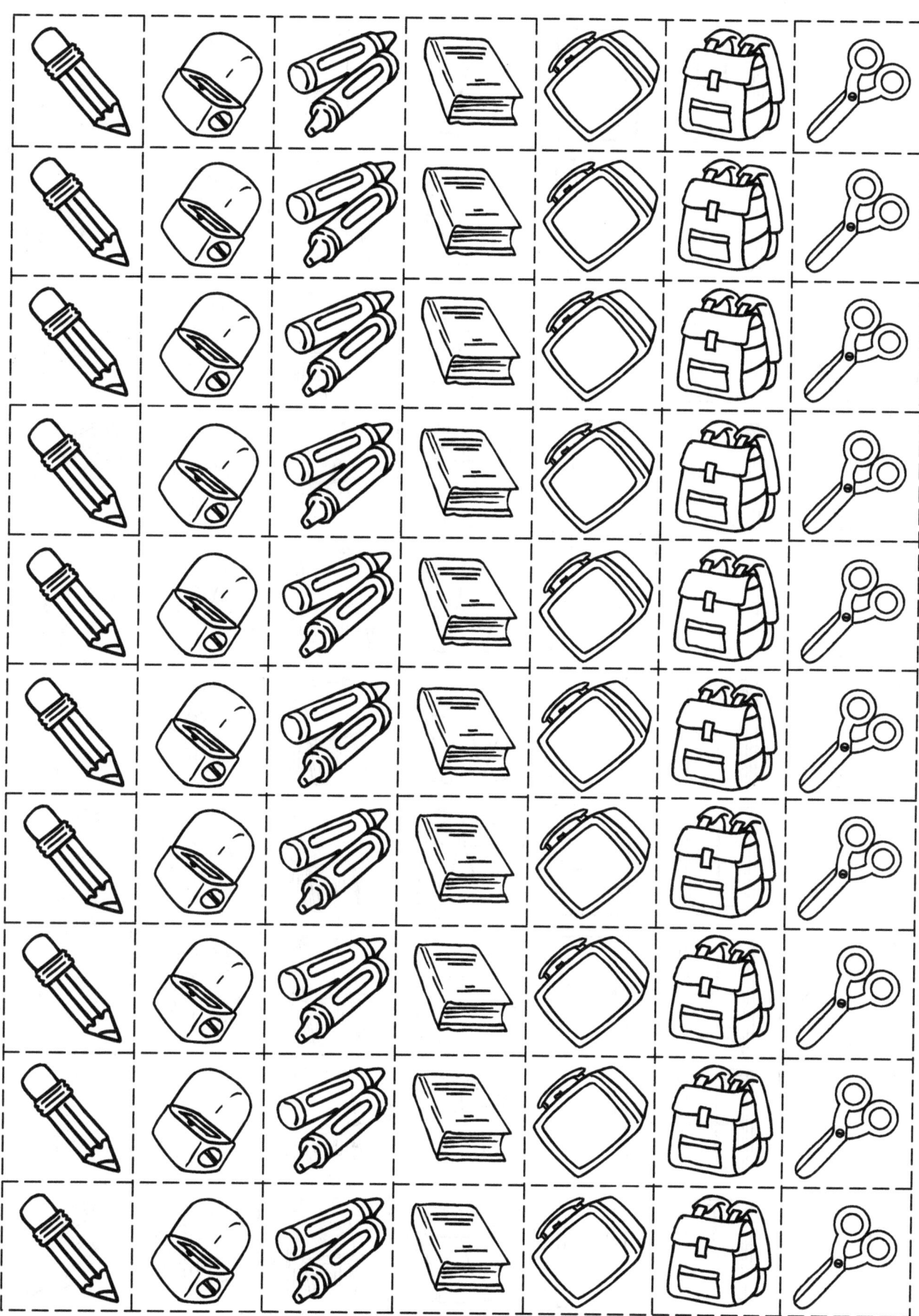

Chart Cards

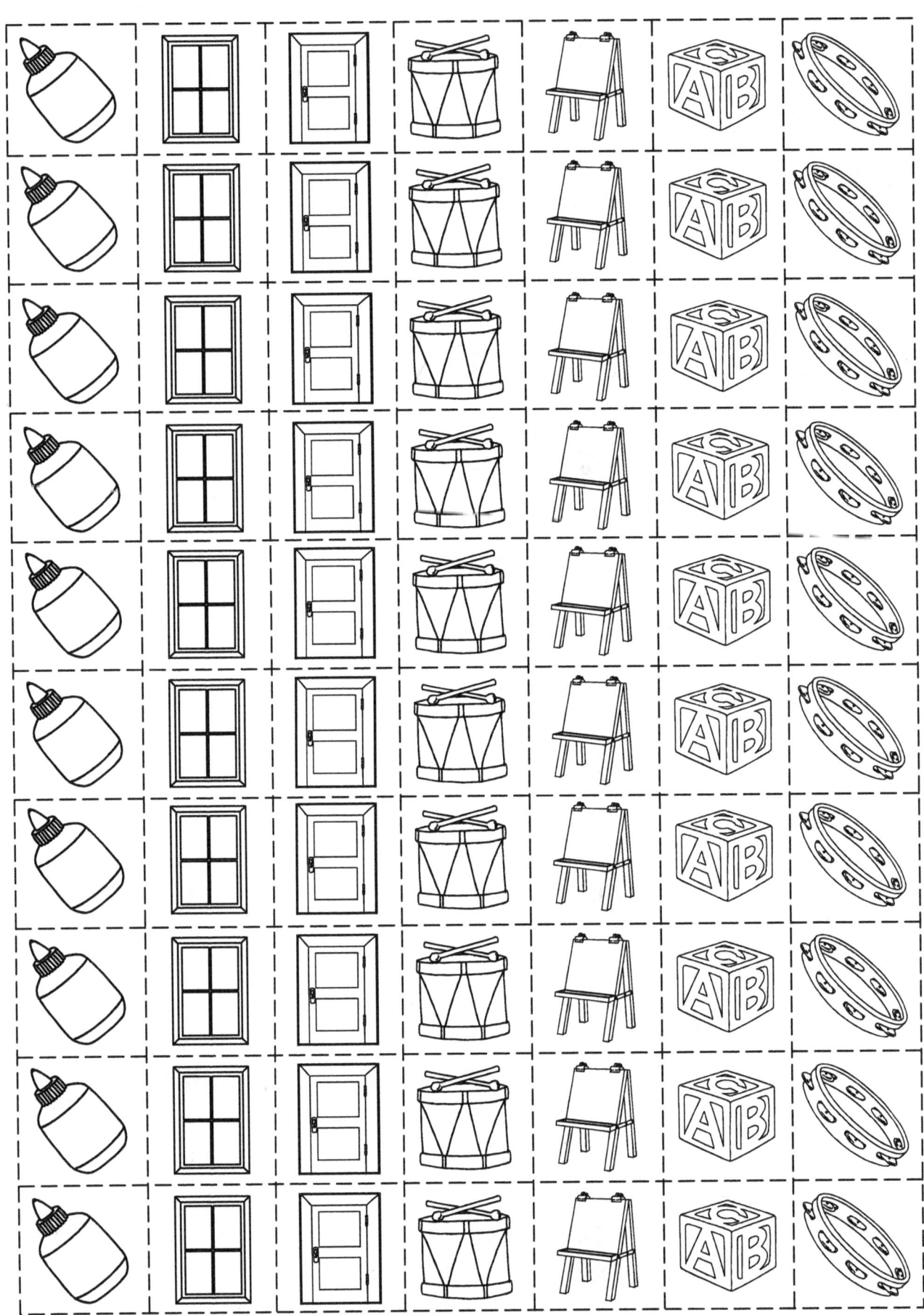

Chart Cards

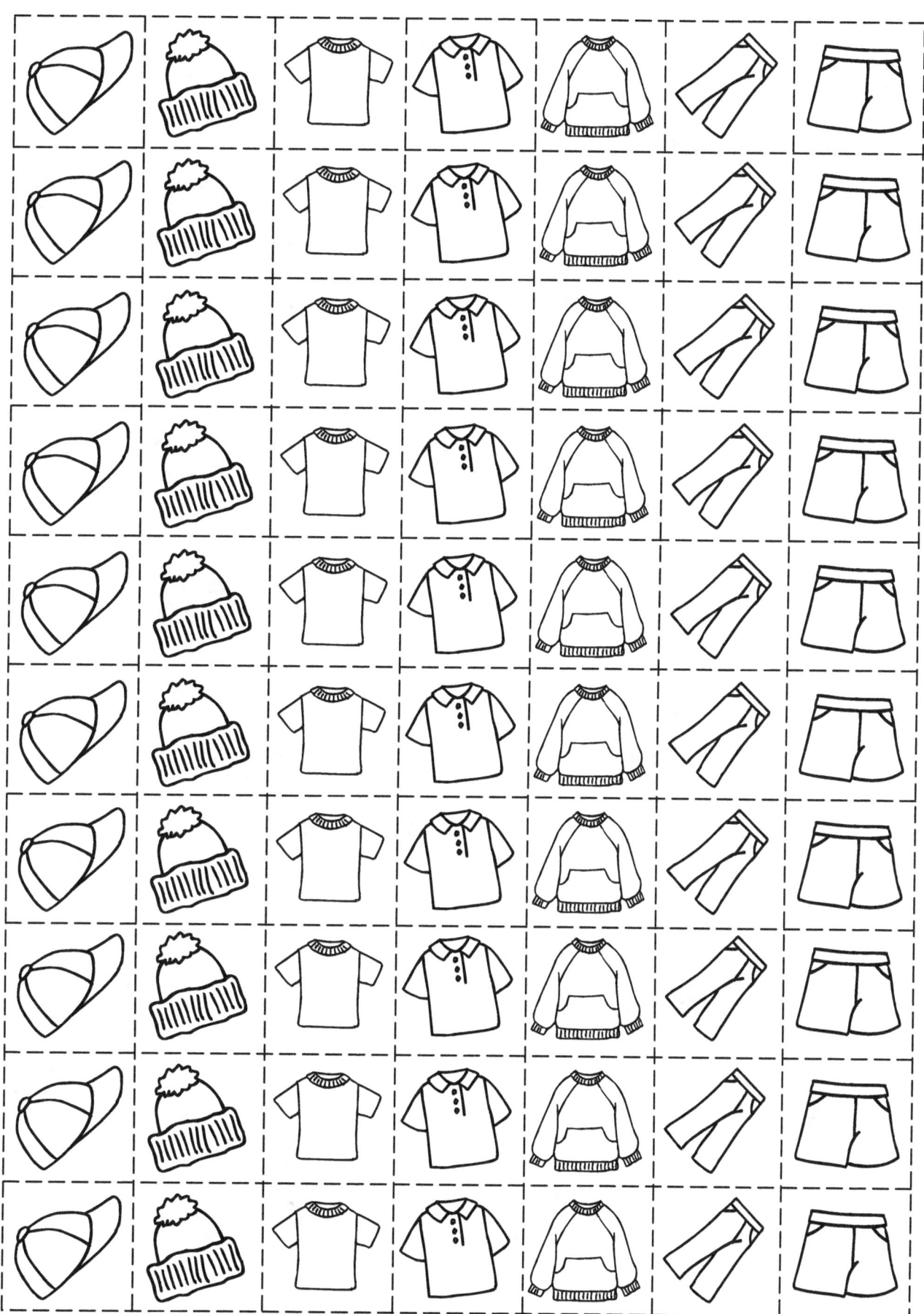

Chart Cards

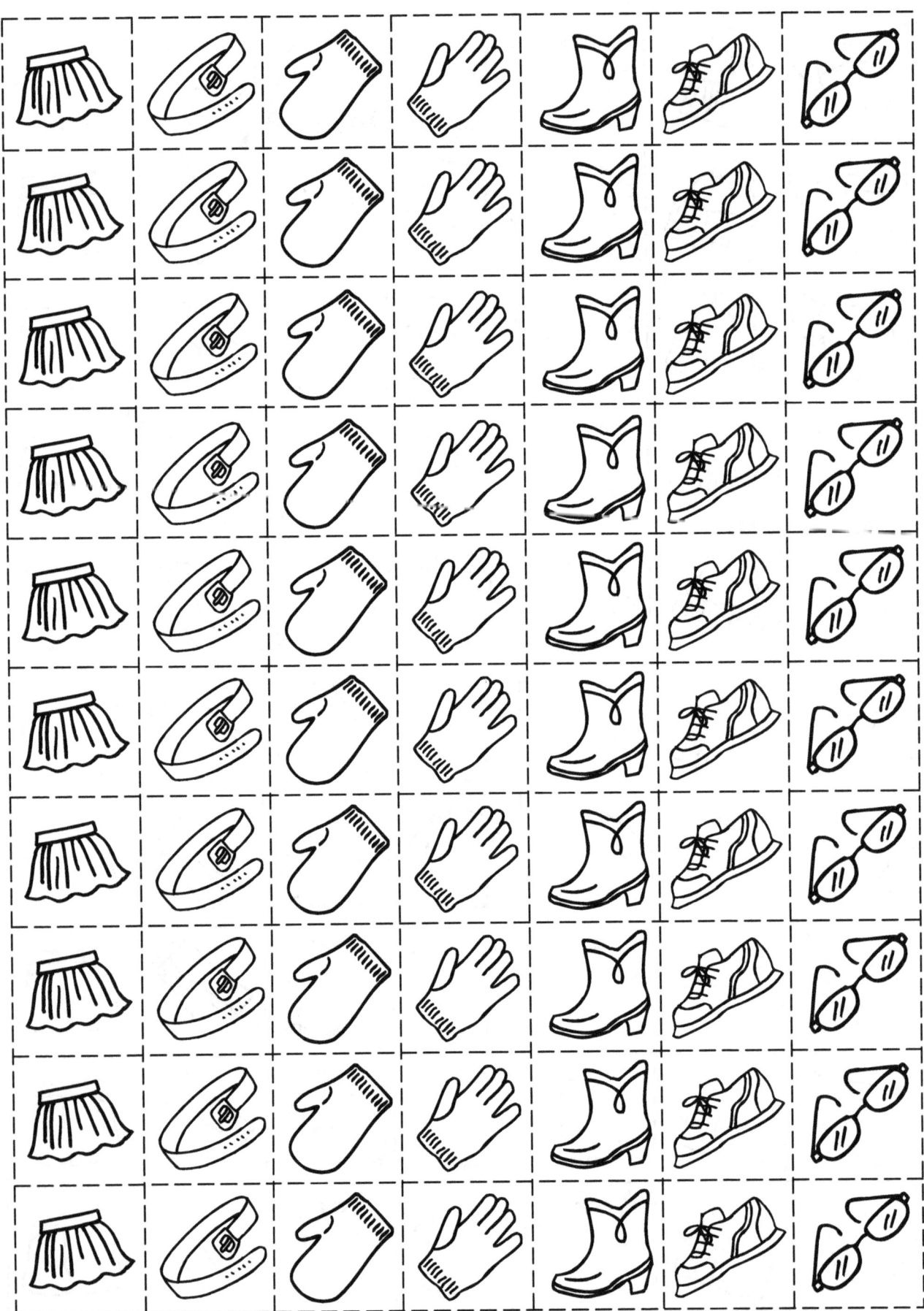

www.ingramcontent.com/pod-product-compliance
Lightning Source LLC
Chambersburg PA
CBHW081020040426
42444CB00014B/3296